Hariette

GW01003780

LOVESTROKES

*Handwriting
Analysis
for
Love, Sex,
and
Compatibility*

PERENNIAL LIBRARY

Harper & Row, Publishers • New York
Cambridge, Philadelphia, San Francisco, Washington
London, Mexico City, São Paulo, Singapore, Sydney

FIRST EDITION

Designed by Ruth Bornschlegel

Library of Congress Cataloging-in-Publication Data

Surovell, Hariette.
   Lovestrokes : handwriting analysis for love, sex, and compatibility.
   Includes index.
   1. Graphology. 2. Love. 3. Sex (Psychology) 4. Interpersonal
relations. I. Title.
BF905.L68S97   1987   155.2'82   86-45698
ISBN 0-06-096141-4 (pbk.)

---

87 88 89 90 91 MPC 10 9 8 7 6 5 4 3 2 1

For my mother, Esther Surovell, a left-handed writer whose right slant and rounded forms reveal her loving heart, generous spirit and infinite capacity for caring

Contents

Acknowledgments

I would like to thank the following people for their help and support:

- Felix Klein and Roger Rubin, my brilliant teachers and lifelong friends
- Janice Bottenus Klein, my fellow pea in the pod
- Janet Goldstein, my inspiring and delightful editor
- Hiroko Kiiffner, my enthusiastic and dedicated agent
- Philip Nobile, who conceptualized the article "Your Sexual Handwriting" for *Forum* magazine
- Jack Heidenry, who suggested that the material in the *Forum* article be expanded into a book
- Linda Peterson, my editor for the *Glamour* article "What a Man's Handwriting Says About His Sexuality"

Additional thanks go to:

- All my wonderful, supportive friends, especially Linsey Abrams and Claire Youmans
- My family
- Zen and Areta Chernyk
- Campus Network and The Source Radio Network
- Christopher Pluck and his crew
- Lou McCulloch
- Livia Sylva Salon
- Café Rapid Algebra
- Indiana Catering
- Dr. Richard Hirsch of New York City, whose chiropractic adjustments made it possible for me to sit comfortably at the typewriter to write this book!

Preface: Getting in the Mood

Your handwriting is a blueprint of your unconscious.

Each time you put pen to paper, you reveal a world of information about your inner needs and your inner life.

Handwriting analysis, or graphology, functions like a magnifying lens. It brings into focus the secrets of your basic character, emotional makeup, intellectual gifts, creative abilities, social adjustment, material values, neurotic conflicts, parental hang-ups, sensuality, sexuality and much, much more.

Analyzing your own handwriting provides you with new self-awareness. Analyzing another person's writing enables you to understand them more accurately. Graphology can show you whether someone will be a sympathetic employer, a loyal friend, an honest business partner, a reliable roommate. In this book, *Lovestrokes,* we will use handwriting analysis for the purpose of evaluating romantic relationships. *Lovestrokes* is for anyone who is looking for love, who is already involved in a romance or marriage, or who wants to know why love remains elusive. *Lovestrokes* is a unique graphological guide to relationships in the eighties.

When we're choosing a mate, our concerns become unique and specific. *Lovestrokes* zeros in on all the areas important to romantic relationships—emotional neediness, romantic nature, sexual style and needs, ability to communicate and compromise, capacity for intimacy, willingness to make a commitment, value systems, honesty and integrity, and hidden troubles—and charms.

Times have changed since the "Ozzie and Harriet" days of the 1950s when people routinely married their high-school sweethearts or their next-door neighbors—and so have romantic priorities. The eighties lover seeks out a supportive soulmate instead of a "good provider." But elevating one's standards complicates rather than simplifies romance. Accepting a date, choosing a mate, maintaining a long-term relationship or a casual affair can prove exhilarating . . . and exasperating.

For Baby Boomers who find dating rituals artificial, a Lovestrokes Analysis will help them to make selective choices.

Teens who are new to the "dating game" will feel less trepidation about the process. A prospective date's penmanship will tell them if he is secretly shy but extremely generous, or whether her reserve conceals oversensitivity.

Engaged couples can use their Lovestrokes Analysis to confirm that they are making a wise decision.

Happily married or cohabitating couples can use graphology to validate old perceptions and learn exciting new secrets about their mate. And since change is an essential aspect of any enduring and dynamic relationship, they will be able to see the subtle ways in which the person they met long ago has grown.

Couples whose relationships are troubled can pinpoint problem areas and expose hidden conflicts to be more readily solved.

Newly single men and women can analyze their exes for a deeper understanding of past relationship patterns.

Users of the personals ads can apply the lessons of *Lovestrokes* to their pursuit of love through letters. Requests for handwritten responses will enable them to screen the "write" date.

Lovestrokes will also provide the reader with new self-understanding. You will be able to pinpoint your romantic behavior patterns, your relationship priorities and your emotional needs.

The final chapter of *Lovestrokes,* "The Lovestrokes Compatibility Questionnaire," is a guide to determining the potential for romantic, sexual and even marital harmony between any two people, based on the complete Lovestrokes Analysis.

In order to benefit fully from a Lovestrokes Analysis, it is necessary to accept the premise that graphology can lead to psychological insight.

Yet many people think that graphology is a game.

In fact, graphology is a science that began its modern development in Europe in the nineteenth century. Today, it is taught in many European universities. Research is being conducted on graphology's potential to diagnose medical problems, including cancer, and to detect evidence of sexual abuse and early childhood trauma in patients under psychological care.

Still, you may wonder, how can so much be contained in one's script? Try thinking about handwriting in a whole new way.

When you were a child, you were probably taught the Palmer method of penmanship in an American grade school. Palmer emphasizes elaborate flourishes, ornate capitals and precise forms. The demand to achieve "perfect Palmer" exasperates some students and challenges others. Finicky teachers may penalize students for their sloppy penmanship, forcing them to stay after class to practice their *p*'s and *q*'s. "Lefties" are often shamed into becoming "righties." And yet there comes a day when every adult has the same experience: we look down at a written page and realize we have created a unique, individualistic, personally expressive handwriting. Chances are good that it bears little resemblance to "perfect Palmer."

Why is this? What happens in between age seven, when you patiently copy the pages of your penmanship workbook, and age seventeen, when you decide that your signature will look more sophisticated if you make it purposely illegible?

The answer is simple—you have grown up, formed a distinct identity and personality, a complex set of values and opinions, ideals and idiosyncracies. Palmer represents the rules and regulations that we were asked to conform to as kids. The specific manner in which we deviate from or adhere to Palmer is a reflection of our adjustment to that upbringing.

Essentially, handwriting expresses the inner self because it is a tool of *dynamics,* similar to speech and to body language. But while we can control our speech and our physical movements, an adult's handwriting can only be changed with great difficulty. One can lie with a straight face, speak warmly to someone detestable, smile while depressed, sing false praises, even fake tears, but it is virtually impossible to consciously alter the width of the right and left margins you make on a page on a sustained basis. The handwriting never lies.

Still skeptical? Ask yourself these questions:

- Have you ever been surprised by someone's handwriting because it seemed so unlike them?
- Has a handwriting ever made you uneasy?
- Do you prefer receiving a handwritten letter because it's more personal?

- Have you ever wondered why some handwritings are very connected and others are a combination of disconnected script and block capitals?

You may be proud of your pretty handwriting, or still embarrassed because it's not perfect Palmer. In either case, you know that your handwriting cannot be duplicated. Like fingerprints, no two are alike.

In the first chapter, we will see why specific graphological indicators have psychological implications. We will learn the rudiments of the graphological analysis. Then we will see how to apply this knowledge to determine romantic compatibility. The lessons of *Lovestrokes* will enable any thoughtful person to make intelligent choices and judgments . . . to seek out their soulmate.

I first became interested in graphology at the age of nineteen, when a stranger at a Manhattan street-fair handwriting analysis booth provided me with uncanny insights into my character on the basis of a page of script. I was so impressed—and intrigued—that I asked where he had learned his craft. He referred me to Felix Klein, America's premier graphologist, the past president of both the National Society for Graphology and the American Association of Handwriting Analysts. I studied with Felix Klein and with his associate, Roger Rubin, president of the National Society for Graphology, for the past ten years. Professional graphology requires such intensive commitment. Both Klein and Rubin have functioned as technical consultants for this book.

The response to the articles on graphology I have written for *Glamour* and *Forum* magazines convinced me that the layperson can master the basic tools of graphology. It is my hope that this knowledge will assist my readers in making intelligent and informed romantic decisions.

Graphology has been invaluable to me in personal relationships. I always obtain a handwriting sample on the first date. After dinner and dancing, I scrutinize the script for its Lovestrokes. Lovestrokes Analyses have helped me to pinpoint many diamonds in the rough. Sometimes, my intuitive perceptions conflicted with my Lovestrokes Analysis. Invariably, subsequent experiences proved that the handwriting was "write"!

LOVESTROKES

1 How to Analyze Handwriting: The Basics

In order to learn about Lovestrokes—those specific aspects of a handwriting that pertain to love relationships—one must first learn the basic techniques of handwriting analysis.

There is a lot of information contained in this chapter. The stereotyped notion that handwriting analysis concerns only the dotting of i's, the crossing of t's, and the signature is completely erroneous. The handwriting's slant, pressure, letter formations, spacing, loops, proportions and many other factors must be appraised in any thorough evaluation.

All the techniques of handwriting analysis—or graphology—that are discussed in this chapter will be reiterated and clarified throughout the book. The basic handwriting analysis provides insight into the writer's personality structure. Then, Lovestrokes Analyses illuminate the writer's romantic, sexual and emotional orientation. The lessons of Lovestrokes will enable you to determine your potential for romantic compatibility with anyone you put to the penmanship test.

THE IDEAL HANDWRITING SAMPLE

The ideal sample consists of two paragraphs of script and a signature written in ballpoint pen on unlined 8½-by-11-inch paper. The two paragraphs will provide sufficient material for an incisive analysis. Ballpoint is essential because—unlike felt-tipped or fountain pens—it shows the degree of pressure used by the writer. Unlined paper allows the writer to create margins and other spatial arrangements.

The content of the sample should be original, not copied. Song lyrics and poetry, arranged line by line, are not acceptable. The surface the paper rests on should be smooth. The writer should be reassured that you will not be judging the sample's content, only its presentation.

At the bottom of the page, ask the writer to indicate his age, sex, and right- or left-handedness. These three factors cannot be surmised through handwriting analysis. Nor can graphology predict the future.

FIRST IMPRESSIONS

You might want to analyze your own handwriting first, to achieve enhanced self-awareness and a possible deeper understanding of your own romantic patterns and priorities.

But let's suppose that you're planning to scrutinize the script of a brand-new acquaintance.

Try to form a "first impression" of the handwriting—in the same way that you form a first impression of someone you meet at a party, based on their appearance, body language, speech patterns and other mannerisms.

Does the handwriting in your sample show creativity? Is it energetic and exuberant? Narrow and cramped? Large and expansive? Chaotic and disorganized? Childish and illegible? Sophisticated and smooth?

In the sample below, we get a first impression of an energetic, outgoing personality.

It is the handwriting of a well-known radio personality.

> *repeating words over & over —*
> *like chanting a mantra.*
> *Banana was an early favorite.*
> *Haile Selassie and Habib*

In the next sample, we get a first impression of a person who is well organized, highly disciplined, creative and artistic.

It is the handwriting of a record industry executive who is also a successful abstract painter.

It was during high school that I made a decision to change my handwriting. I had a classmate in my senior year whose writing style I admired. At the time, my own style was "irregularly elongated mutant Palmer," and I had grown embarrassed of it. Concurrently, I had

Both of those samples contain letter formations that are much different from the Palmer—or schooltype—method of penmanship taught to American children.

SCHOOLTYPE VERSUS CREATIVE

Typically, "nonconformists," artistic people and independent thinkers develop handwritings that bear little resemblance to the schooltype model. People who are still influenced by a conservative upbringing, or who prefer being conventional and fear going against the grain, will show more of the schooltype influence.

This handwriting, by a female beautician, is an example of a schooltype writing.

be analyzing my handwriting in your book, Love Strokes, to be published by Harper & Row,

This handwriting, by a female astrologer, is an example of a creative writing.

Agrigius, who was married to Agrippa, had no sons, but had other one daughter

A strong schooltype influence does not imply that the writer is less complicated, opinionated or intelligent than a creative writer. But because the letters in schooltype writing are well connected, there is a tendency toward using logic instead of intuition.

LOGIC VERSUS INTUITION

Most creative handwritings show a combination of block capitals and block letters, and the letters in words are often disconnected. This is a sign of intuitive thinking.

Strongly connected letters show a linear, step-by-step thought process. Letters that are both connected and disconnected show that the writer relies on intuitive impressions.

Here are illustrations of two intelligent writers who think in very different ways. The first—the intuitive thinker—is a record company publicist who must use instinctive reasoning and quick judgments on the job. The second—the logical thinker—is a lawyer and corporate vice-president who thinks carefully before making any verbal commitments.

getting married. Old friends, new

Highly Intuitive

is to assume that the world is a nail -- and I am a hammer.

Cautious, Logical Reasoning

SIMPLIFICATION

Few people write perfect schooltype as adults. The reason for this is that the ornate and elaborate capitals of the schooltype model are too time-consuming to form. Therefore, most handwritings will show elements of simplification—which means that they eliminate frivolous flourishes. In the sample demonstrating intuitive thinking, we see that the writer uses block capitals and highly simplified, practically printed small letters. This shows incisive intelligence and also individualism, because it differs so dramatically from schooltype.

In the sample demonstrating logical thinking, we find that the letters are also simplified, showing incisive intelligence, but their schooltype-styled formations reveal a more conventional personality.

When a handwriting shows a combination of schooltype capitals and simplified capitals, it means that the writer's values are undergoing a transformation.

In the following sample, the capital *G* is strongly schooltype, while the capital *V* is simplified, indicating that this aspiring actress retains many of her parents' values, and rejects just as many.

Simplified and Schooltype Capitals

SLANT

Think about meeting people at a party. Let's say a stranger approaches you and begins a conversation. If you like this person and want to get to know him, you will lean forward in his direction to make closer contact.

If you're unsure about whether you like or dislike him, you'll stand in a formal, self-contained pose.

If you want to be left alone, you will lean away from him.

In the same way, the slant of a handwriting shows how a person relates to others—whether he is an extrovert, an introvert or a combination of tendencies.

Slant includes four basic categories: *right slant, extreme right slant, vertical* and *left slant*. The following examples show illustrations of each.

RIGHT SLANT

Writing that slants to the right shows extroversion. The right slant writer reaches out to others, is sensitive, empathic and aims to please. A right slant is a sign of a sociable nature.

> *Points. Brownie Points is a dessert Cafe in the east village.*
> *Tom is grey and white and he also has green eyes.*

Right Slant

EXTREME RIGHT SLANT

Writing that slants excessively to the right shows insecurity and a tendency toward emotional dependency, because the writer "leans too far" toward others. The extreme right slant writer needs to be liked. The ego is weak, and the person may do anything for approval. Therefore, social judgment may be poor.

> *look for a way to start the day getting things in proportion spread the news and help the world go around.*

Extreme Right Slant

VERTICAL

Vertical writing shows poise and self-containment. Usually, people who use vertical writing were oversensitive children who often got their feelings hurt. They learned to develop control over their emotions and will not easily reveal their true feelings. Because they are socially savvy, vertical writers have needs for partying as well as for privacy.

> *What can I possibly find out about myself, that I don't already know, through handwriting analysis?*

Vertical

LEFT SLANT

Writing that slants to the left may simply show that the writer is left-handed. In that case, other graphological indicators will reveal the writer's sociability. ∞

When a right-handed writer uses a left slant, it is a sign of introversion. The left slant writer reveals his "true self" to only a few select people—only after they have passed a long series of critical "tests."

Left-Handed Left Slant

Right-Handed Left Slant

Over the course of a day, your handwriting may show shifts in slant, an indication of changing moods. For instance, a vertical writer returning from a convivial lunch with co-workers may show some right slant tendencies. If, an hour later, she has an unpleasant confrontation with her boss, her writing will slant more toward the left. But, in both cases, it will still be essentially vertical.

DEPRESSION AND OPTIMISM

Whatever your slant category, its direction on the page will tell whether you're feeling pessimistic—and depressed, or optimistic—and upbeat.

In the two samples at the top of page 24, the uphill direction shows optimism, the downhill direction shows depression.

Because direction is so dependent on the writer's mood, it can change dramatically from one day to the next.

You can hear calypso songs everywhere — in clubs, on beaches, in hotels and at parties. Calypso is the lively voice of a lively people

Optimism

Working with a record Company is at times exciting, but most

Depression

OTHER SLANT FACTORS

While slant is an important key to the writer's emotional nature, it does not provide a definitive picture of his social interactions. In the handwriting that illustrated right slant, we can see clearly that the writer leaves wide spaces between words. This is a sign that although he wants to make contact with others, he finds it difficult to bridge the emotional gap.

Points. Brownie Points is a dessert Cafe in the east village.

Right Slant, Wide Spaces Between Words

In subsequent chapters, the many implications of the writer's use of space will be explored. This will include space between words, between letters, between lines, and the right and left margins.

CONNECTIVE FORM

Surprisingly, the manner in which writers form their small *m*'s, *n*'s and *h*'s is extremely significant. There are five categories of connective forms: the *schoolmodel,* the *garland,* the *arcade,* the *angle* and the *thread.*

THE SCHOOLMODEL

The schoolmodel form shows a need to appear conventional, even at the cost of self-expression.

generous. Right now he's working for Random House publishers, which he does

THE GARLAND

The presence of garland formations shows a flexible, adaptable, pleasure-loving, gentle, kind and "open" nature.

remember as a child

THE ARCADE

The tightly wound arcade formation shows emotional restriction; the result of an upbringing in which correct social behavior was stressed. Arcades are also used by "visual" people—like artists and architects.

warm day of March

THE ANGLE

The rigid angle formation shows a domineering, uncompromising, strong-willed and controlling nature. Angle writers think they know what is best for others and like to give orders. The angle formation is also a sign of superb discipline and organization.

*The summer is hot in New York
The people are tiresome / Our third*

THE THREAD

The loose and easy thread formation is made by people who are unconventional, intuitive, freedom-loving and possibly neurotic. Thread writers can "see through" people and are therefore capable of skillful manipulation. They also have the ability to understand "both sides to every story" and may willingly switch their stance. Threads can show creative simplification or impatience.

Speedy Thread Form

Creative and Simplified Thread Form

ROUNDEDNESS VERSUS ANGULARITY

When a relationship is filled with conflict, we say that it is "rocky." Rocks are hard, angular objects.

A couple enjoying an easy rapport says that their relationship is "smooth sailing." Waves are rounded and flowing.

In handwriting, rounded formations show a capacity for emotional release. Angular formations show the attempt at emotional control. Roundedness shows a feeling, empathic nature. A lack of roundedness, or angularity, shows a conflicted, frustrated nature.

The following is an example of a rounded writing.

The Liberty Hotel at 805 Washington Street, like so many other center city residential hotels, was on the edge of extinction. But unlike

Rounded Writing

Here is an example of an angular writing.

telephone. But ATT put an end to that. Now what will the lovers do. They can't smoke — it'll kill you. So they say. As far as I

Angular Writing

Naturally, not every writing will be entirely rounded or entirely angular. In the next example, wide, rounded loops and other rounded forms co-exist with angular connective forms and angular letter formations. This indicates that the writer has lots of feelings and emotional needs, but his inner tension and psychological conflicts inhibit his self-expression.

When it's apple blossom time in Orange New Jersey, we'll be a peach of a pear. Though we can't elope, honey — do be mine

Rounded and Angular Writing

THE THREE ZONES AND THE BASE LINE

Many psychologists and psychiatrists employ a diagnostic test called the "Tree test." The patient is asked to draw a tree. The resulting picture symbolizes his psychological makeup. The tree trunk represents the patient's ego. The branches—which are "reaching to the sky"—portray dreams, goals and aspirations. The ground is the tree's foundation, and the patient's emotional stability. The roots are "what's beneath" and thus the unconscious.

The three zones of handwriting can be directly compared to the tree test.

Here is an illustration of the three zones. Every letter you write will span at least one of the zones.

BASE LINE

UPPER ZONE
MIDDLE ZONE
LOWER ZONE

The upper zone represents the areas symbolized by the branches. The middle zone is the tree trunk. The base line—the horizontal line a sentence is written on—is the ground. The lower zone contains the roots.

The upper zone includes the tops of all capital letters and the tops of the small letters *b, d, f, h, k, l* and *t*. The height and shape of the upper zone formations symbolize the writer's ambitions, spirituality, ideals and intellectualism.

The middle zone is used in every letter. Middle zone small letters are *a, c, e, i, m, n, o, r, s, u, v, w* and *x*. The size, legibility, connective form and other formations in the middle zone symbolize the writer's ego and self-esteem, sense for reality, daily functioning and material interests.

The base line is formed by connecting the lowest point of each middle zone letter. It is the barometer of emotional stability, and the division between the conscious and the unconscious mind.

The lower zone includes the lower loops of the small letters *f, q, j, p, y* and *z*. These loops—or other formations—symbolize the writer's instinctual drives, sexual impulses, unconscious desires and body image.

Ideally, a handwriting would have balance and proportion between the three zones. The first sample on the opposite page is an example of a well-balanced handwriting—and, therefore, an emotionally well-adjusted person.

Neglect—or poorly formed letters—in one of the zones shows problems in that area. In the next example, a virtually illegible middle zone shows a weak ego.

An overemphasis on a zone shows the writer's priorities. For instance, in the example below, the writer overemphasizes his upper zone to compensate for his neglected middle zone. We can conclude that he believes that fulfilling his high ambitions will give him the ego strength that he lacks.

Confusion between the zones, or zone interference, usually means a confusion in the writer's value system. At the bottom of the page is an example of zone confusion—many of the upper zone formations stay in the middle zone.

I love my job because I am surrounded by people with smiles all day long. The

Balance Between the Three Zones

Sample in years. I find first easier dance that lost a cigarette.

Middle Zone Neglect

but I don't use it that

Overemphasized Upper Zone

rang, and it was the postoffice calling to tell

Zone Interference

EXTREMES

Any extreme letter formations in the handwriting will reveal problems.

If the extreme appears in the upper zone, it could mean problems fulfilling ambitions.

I saw your Casting in The New York magazine

Upper Zone Extremes

If the extreme appears in the lower zone, it usually means sexual frustration.

trip to Denver as exciting as

Lower Zone Extreme

An extremely large capital *I* is a sign of insecurity, not confidence. A confident person forms a moderate-sized capital *I*. An extremely small capital *I* also shows a poor self-image.

I can remember

Extremely Large Capital I

I feel instinctively

Extremely Small Capital I

REGULARITY

Regularity in handwriting is seen when the letter formations are consistent. A writing need not show a schooltype influence to be considered regular—highly creative and simplified handwritings can show equal regularity.

Regularity is a reflection of the writer's emotional stability. Good regularity shows maturity and dependability.

Here is an example of a regular handwriting.

When my daddy comes home, he's going to buy me everything

Good Regularity

Irregularity is seen when the letter formations are constantly changing. Irregularity can mean that the writer is unpredictable—or emotionally unstable.

Here is an example of an irregular handwriting.

let go of the stress of daily life and just slide back into/onto

Irregularity

THE SIGNATURE

Your signature represents the image you present to the world. In a thorough handwriting analysis, the signature should be compared—for its form, size and legibility—to the rest of the handwriting sample.

If the signature is similar in form, size and legibility to the rest of the handwriting, it shows an up-front, down-to-earth and secure person.

Underlinings, flourishes and other embellishments show insecurity. So does a disproportionately large signature.

Some people believe that an illegible signature is a sign of sophistication. But, in many cases, an illegible signature shows that the writer wants to appear elusive and mysterious.

If the first name is very distant from the surname, or disproportionate in size, it can mean ambivalent feelings about one's family—or, in the case of a divorced woman, her ex-husband.

Since celebrities are constantly asked for autographs, their signatures may be the most significant aspect of their handwriting.

And those are the techniques of basic handwriting analysis. We will be focusing on all these graphological indicators when we look at the Lovestrokes in the handwriting. Each Lovestrokes Analysis must be evaluated along with the other graphological indicators.

Here is a handwriting analysis of a twenty-seven-year-old salesman.

> A few months ago, I'm on my way to a cheap lunch on 18th St and I see two old Jewish businessmen on the sidewalk arguing in sign language. Watching for a few moments, they became more and more animated as the argument got more and more heated.
>
> Now I'm not literate in sign language but just in the way they were moving their hands and arms, I swear I could see the accent.

The angular connective forms in this handwriting might lead you to conclude that the writer is rigid and unyielding. Yet, rounded forms and large lower loops indicate that he has a great deal of feeling and lots of emotional needs. His right slant shows sensitivity to others. A clear middle zone shows good self-esteem. Therefore, angular forms are probably the result of tension and frustration. In a relationship with an empathic and caring woman, he would prove to be supportive, warm and nurturing.

The basic handwriting analysis is the key to the writer's personality. Lovestrokes Analyses will help you to determine romantic compatibility potential—whether you're looking for a casual date or a lifelong mate!

2 The Intimacy Factor

In an article in the September 1986 issue of Psychology Today *called "The Three Faces of Love," Dr. Robert Sternberg of Yale University describes "complete love" as consisting of "commitment, passion and intimacy."*

The dictionary definition of intimacy is "something private and personal, deep and thorough." In a love relationship, intimacy entails sharing your most private feelings, your deepest fears, your most personal needs.

Naturally, intimacy requires trust, which doesn't develop automatically. People are so complicated that their outer personas often can be misleading.

A pretty girl who seems stuck-up and snobby may be pathologically shy. The guy who is the life of the party could be covering up his insecurity.

Falling in love makes understanding someone even more difficult. When we become infatuated, we want our lover's esteem and approval. We show them our best sides, and vice versa. We may even try to "become" the person they would like us to be. Some couples avoid revealing any negative character traits for months. Eventually, though, as a relationship progresses, both partners tend to worry less about making a good impression and concentrate more on getting their needs met. Ironically, just when you are starting to trust someone, you may discover that they are quite different than you originally believed.

Let's explore a hypothetical situation.* Ron was an ambitious investment banker whose major goal in life was to become a millionaire. When he met Nicole, she impressed him as being the ultimate "eighties woman"—capable, confident and self-assured. Six months into their relationship, Nicole began calling Ron at his office several times a day, asking his opinion on everything from whether she should take a dance class after work to the advisability of writing a memo to her boss. It wasn't long before Ron broke off the

**Note:* All anecdotes in this book are fictitious, including the names.

relationship, wondering, "How could she have fooled me so long about what she was really like?"

Throughout their year-long engagement, Mike seemed as eager as Moira to talk through any misunderstandings, to verbalize both affection and anger. After they were married, such sensitivity sessions came to an abrupt halt. Whenever Moira summoned up the nerve to interrupt Mike while he polished the car, rewired lamps and tinkered with the stereo system to say, "When are we gonna talk about us, honey?" he would angrily reply, "All you ever want to do is sit around talking about your feelings! Can't you see I'm busy?"

In divorce court, Moira told her sister, "I married a stranger."

If Ron and Moira had studied up on their Lovestrokes, they would have been able to assess their partner's needs for intimacy and communication. The graphological indicators of slant, roundedness, connective forms and zone emphasis all shed light on the writer's emotional nature.

However, a person's "true" emotional nature is not always consistent with his or her behavior.

Commonly, people suppress or repress their needs, or establish a strict set of priorities based on their life experiences.

For instance, let's say that the "real" emotional nature of a middle-aged single woman is highly sensitive and empathic. Logically, she would desire honest, intimate connections in her romantic relationships.

But if, in the past, both friends and lovers took advantage of this woman's good nature by constantly asking for favors and then refusing her own—infrequent—requests for help, she might develop a protective shell. She might seek out superficial, shallow relationships with inappropriate mates—anything to avoid reexperiencing the pain of vulnerability.

If this woman meets a man who is also tenderhearted, nurturing and sympathetic, she might initially be mistrustful. Her suspicion may cause her to "test" him out, let's say by making a public scene, to challenge him to prove his sincerity. Maybe he'll pass her tests; maybe he'll be disappointed in her and abandon the relationship.

Or take a teenaged boy whose "real" emotional nature—open and expressive—has caused him pain throughout his life. As a child, he cried easily, and was taunted by the neighborhood kids who called him a "sissy." When his first girlfriend left him for another, he was devastated—so his best friend called him a "wimp." Now, when he takes a girl out on a date, he *plays the part of a cool, confident and even cruel "macho man." Deep inside, he's praying that he won't be hurt again.*

The "real" emotional nature is established in early childhood. The unique and individualistic way in which a person adapts to his or her emotional nature is one of the most important aspects of Lovestrokes. It tells you if the writer embraces intimacy or repels attempts at intimacy . . . wallows in emotional expression or has decided that matters of the head take precedence over matters of the heart.

Determining the intimacy factor will show you the ease—or the obstacles—in establishing an emotional rapport with the writer of your handwriting sample. This is the first step in determining your romantic compatibility potential.

THE USE OF SPACE

In order to see how the writer's emotional nature is manifested in his or her social behavior, we must examine the writer's use of *space*—space between words, space between letters, space between lines and the right and left margins.

Think for a moment about the symbolism of the use of space. When we are desirous of privacy and solitude, we say that we need some "personal space." When someone breathes on our food or takes up too much elbow room, we say that they "violate our personal space." In their classic song "Don't Stand So Close to Me," the Police made a statement about the need for physical and psychic space.

If a page filled with handwriting functions as a microcosm of the writer's world—revealing the inner life and the outer behavior—then spaces show the psychic space the writer maintains in relationships.

SPACES BETWEEN WORDS

Spaces between words directly represent the psychic and physical space the writer maintains between himself and others—the willingness to be close or the need to maintain distance. They can be *wide and even, extremely wide, narrow and even* and *narrow and uneven.*

When the spaces between words are wide and even, it shows that the writer is thoughtful and organized when writing, because such spatial organization requires intuitive aesthetic judgment. Therefore, such spacing shows deep feelings, a poetic nature, a sense for beauty and social poise. Such writers know how to maintain the appropriate social "distance"—though they will be more introverted than extroverted.

So how was your vacation??

It warms my heart to

Wide, Even Spaces Between Words

However, extremely wide spaces between words are a strong indication of introversion. The writer places much distance between himself and others, and, as a result, feels emotionally isolated. Childhood trauma is usually a factor in this particular use of space. Even when a person acts in an outgoing manner, like the waitress in the sample below, the "real self" is inward.

Can tell me a few things

I don't already know.

Extremely Wide Spaces Between Words

Narrow, even spaces between words show the desire to reach out to others and a sociable, outgoing nature. Such spacing is the manifestation of a fluid, uncensored and spontaneous flow of writing. Because the spaces are narrow, the writer finds it easy to get close to others, and the evenness of the spaces means that the social judgment is good.

hand-writing analysis. It is also rather difficult to concentrate while listening to two conversations; it is impossible to be

Narrow, Even Spaces Between Words

Finally, narrow, uneven spaces between words indicate a need to be close to people combined with poor social judgment. Such a writing is often an indication of talkativeness.

Narrow, Uneven Spaces Between Words

Graphologically speaking, wide letter formations—be they individual letters, or parts of loops—indicate emotional need and a lack of restraint. Narrow letter formations—letters or loops—reveal inhibition, constriction and restraint. This assumption is similar to the conclusions we make about people based on their physiology. If someone is overweight, we suspect that they use food as a substitute for emotional or sexual fulfillment—and big girth implies that, instead of dieting, they give in to their impulses to eat. A skinny person, on the other hand, practices self-control and restraint in denying himself food.

When we look at the spaces between letters, we must judge the width of the letters to determine the degree of emotional need, and compare that to the amount of distance the writer allots himself in venting emotional expression. In other words, you can see if the writer gives himself a "long leash" or a "short leash"—a large space or a narrow space—when it comes to self-control.

SPACES BETWEEN LETTERS

The categories of spaces between letters include *wide letters, narrow spaces; wide letters, wide spaces; narrow letters, narrow spaces* and *narrow letters, wide spaces.*

In the case of wide letters, narrow spaces, we see that the writer has great emotional needs but doesn't give himself enough "space" to express his feelings, most likely out of the fear that revealing neediness will lead to vulnerability.

first warm day of March

Wide Letters, Narrow Spaces

When letters are wide, and spaces are wide, the writer has lots of feelings and can express them easily, without restraint.

personalities). We make good wives, great mothers)

Wide Letters, Wide Spaces

When letters are narrow and spaces are narrow, the writer is shy and inhibited.

reveals an interesting neighbor

Narrow Letters, Narrow Spaces

But when the letters are narrow, and the spaces are wide, it means that the writer tries to appear emotional and warm, but is actually emotionally self-conscious.

the sea and most of all reaching out for life.

Narrow Letters, Wide Spaces

Now, let's look at the *arrangement of space* on the page.

Pretend that the blank sheet of paper you are presented with is an empty living room.

How will you decorate it?

Will your style be sparse and tasteful? This might mean that you like order and simplicity in your life.

Will you cram furniture into every nook and cranny and plaster each inch of wall space with posters and paintings? In that case, it's quite likely that you need a lot of security, and that surrounding yourself with familiar possessions gives you a feeling of comfort.

Your judgment is also reflected in your decorating style. Too much clutter can mean poor judgment, and could be symptomatic of an inner feeling of chaos. Neatly arranged furniture can be an indication of good judgment, orderliness and self-control.

When presented with a sheet of blank paper, the writer is presented with the challenge of "decorating" it. He consciously chooses the left and right margins, and unconsciously chooses the space between lines.

LEFT AND RIGHT MARGINS

With every line we write, we return to the left margin. For this reason, the left margin represents the conscious image we wish to present to others—as well as our feelings about the past.

The right margin shows our ability to truly reach out to others, as well as our feelings about the future.

Both left and right margins can be consistent in width, or can fluctuate. The categories of margins include: *wide, even left margins; widening left margins; narrowing left margins; narrow left margins; wide right margins; narrow right margins* and *widening right margins.*

Wide, even left margins are an indication of cultural sophistication, self-respect, high standards and formal manners, and good organizational abilities.

handwriting. I adopted these two influences to begin creating a hybrid style of my own. Along the way, I would notice interesting capitals or various other attractive elements in the handwriting of others. After years of borrowings and casting-off, I settled into my current style. All told, the process took about a decade of deliberate fine-tuning.

Wide, Even Left Margin

A widening left margin, one that grows progressively larger, shows that the writer can be carried away by enthusiasm or impatience and may be lavish and extravagant.

Widening Left Margin

A narrowing left margin shows an unsuccessful fight against pride and shyness, caution and prudence. In this case, the writer exerts control over the initial spontaneous impulse.

Narrowing Left Margin

A consistently narrow left margin shows a reluctance to readily expose the "true" self.

Consistently Narrow Left Margin

A wide right margin indicates reserve, oversensitivity, a fear of intimacy, or unwillingness to face reality and the future.

Wide Right Margin

A narrow right margin, on the other hand, shows that the writer moves boldly forward without fear, inhibition or self-restraint. Therefore, this writer faces reality, is optimistic about the future, possesses vitality, may be hasty and embraces intimacy with others.

Narrow Right Margin

Last in this category, a widening right margin is the result of a writer who censors his initial friendly and spontaneous impulses.

Fear of others, shyness and suspicion are evident here.

Widening Right Margin

SPACES BETWEEN LINES

Finally, let's look at the *spaces between lines*. Because a paragraph should ideally contain enough space for the three zones to be proportionately depicted, spaces between lines tell us about clarity in values, as well as judgment, aesthetic sense, organizational abilities, inhibitions and capacity for intimacy. Spaces between lines include *wide, even spaces; extremely wide spaces* and *narrow spaces*.

Wide, even spaces between lines show an analytical mind, good organization, good social judgment, idealism, confidence in one's own logical abilities and social savvy.

your book will instrumental in helping many people to a fuller realization of their sexual potential & love potential

Wide, Even Spaces Between Lines

But extremely wide spaces between lines can mean fear of intimacy, confusion and insecurity about one's own logical abilities . . . or the need to remain remote.

As soon as I walked in the door, after having just

Extremely Wide Spaces Between Lines

Narrow spaces between lines show poor judgment, an emphasis on practicality rather than on aesthetics and a love of sensation. It can also be an indication of identity problems and confusion in values—because the zones interfere.

Our anniversary is in june which will make three years that [we] have been together. [We] gone through a lot of misery but there has also been a lot of love and happiness. If [I've] got anything to do with it [well].

Narrow Spaces Between Lines

Now, let's use our knowledge of the meanings of spacing to draw some conclusions about romantic compatibility.

Are you a single mother of two who needs lots of private time to write in your journal, meditate and just daydream? A writer who leaves wide, even spaces between words will understand that requirement, and will respect your desire to be alone. Intuitively, he will know when you need privacy, and because he needs privacy himself, you will be on each other's wavelength.

But if the writing of the man you admire shows an extreme right slant (emotional dependency), wide loops (emotional neediness) and narrow, even spaces between words (talkativeness), his understanding of your need for solitude will probably be superseded by his constant need for contact, reassurance and intimacy. So when you're off to the attic to listen to your Walkman, he'll be sulking in the cellar, feeling abandoned.

Are you a thirty-seven-year-old nature lover who dreams of marrying an earth mother and moving to a remote country cabin where you can grow your own vegetables and take daily hikes through the woods? Then you should look for a lady garland writer (love of nature) who sustains extremely wide spaces between words (introversion and emotional isolation). If you meet someone who tells you over tea that your plans sound idyllic, but her writing shows narrow, uneven spaces between words . . . then she's fooling you and deluding herself.

While her wide left margins show that she has the organizational ability and discipline to create a prosperous garden, the spacing between words guarantees that—deprived of a group of girlfriends to gossip with—this Vermont Maid would soon start talking to the trees.

Do you suspect that the Robert Redford lookalike who works in the personnel department of your company is secretly shy? If his words contain narrow letters and narrow spaces between letters, then he will probably appreciate your lunch invitation. Be forewarned, however, that if he has a wide right margin (fear of intimacy), he might not really open up to you until Lunch Number Ten. His shyness is practically pathological.

Are you frustrated because your fiancée rarely tells you how much she loves you? If her letters are wide, and the spaces between them are narrow, and if she maintains a widening right margin, then don't take it personally. Judge her by her actions rather than her words, because shyness and oversensitivity cause her to censor her self-expression. Prove to her that she can trust you, that the gamut of her feelings are acceptable to you, and eventually she'll open up.

If you're an ambitious executive who requires a mate who can be depended upon to make gracious conversation at business functions; who is a social asset rather than a liability, then make sure that his writing shows a right slant (desire to please); a wide, even left margin (cultural sophistication, good manners); and wide, even spaces between lines (good social adjustment). If both left and right margins are narrow, and there are narrow spaces between lines (poor judgment), then it's inevitable that even with the best of intentions, this man will make more than his fair share of faux pas.

Does your steady boyfriend advocate the importance of talking about feelings . . . while lending all his lip service to sports? Look first to the loops. If you detect full loops in the upper and lower zones, combined with rounded forms in the middle zone, his intentions are sincere. He may be avoiding initiating emotional interchanges because he is still smarting from his last relationship—the one in which he opened up and told the woman he was living with all his secret fears and insecurities, and she exploited this knowledge when their affair ended. The resulting fear of intimacy will be indicated by the extremely wide right margin that is inconsistent with his right slant (fear of intimacy contradicted by basic sensitivity).

If, on the other hand, your boyfriend's writing shows an absence of loops in all zones, extremely wide spaces between words, an overemphasis in the upper zone and narrow letters with wide spaces between words, then don't expect him to turn off the soccer game every time you want to discuss your anxieties. This Romeo intellectualizes his feelings and would rather not be bothered with emotional demands.

Do you have a crush on a woman who intimidates you because she appears to be rigidly self-controlled? If her writing is rounded and shows wide loops and vertical writing, then her rigidity comes from an attempt to control her intense emotions. Pursue her if she also has a widening left margin—eventually, she will let her impulses triumph over her inhibition.

Slant, roundedness, loops, connective form and the many elements of spacing—all comprise the Lovestrokes that tell you if you and your partner or your prospective partner will be emotionally synchronized . . . or emotionally polarized.

Lovestrokes will show you whether you and yours will have a "failure to communicate" or an enduring communications capacity.

3 *Romance Ratings: What's Your "Lovestyle"?*

Are you an incurable romantic? Do you require twilight, moonlight and candlelight on a date?

Or have you been burned in a love affair, causing your feelings about romance to be more cynical than sentimental?

Most people are raised to believe that one day they will meet that special someone with whom they'll walk on the beach, walk down the aisle and live happily ever after. Lucky lovers fulfill that dream, and manage to keep romance alive in their relationships.

Others keep "looking for love in all the wrong places." So they convince themselves that romantic fantasies are "kid stuff."

Whether you're single or coupled, you probably have thought about your own needs for romance. You could be involved in a long-term relationship that seems to consist of all practical routines and no fun. You could be terminally single and starved for wining, dining and dancing till dawn. Or you could be fortunate enough to have a mate who never comes home from work without a bunch of flowers—even after twenty-five years of marriage!

Generally speaking, the writer who "lives for love" will have a rounded, flowing handwriting. Rounded writers succumb more easily to feelings and fantasies, including romantic fantasies.

Angular writers are more interested in control than spontaneity, which may inhibit their romantic interests.

But that doesn't mean that every rounded writer is incurably romantic, or that the presence of angular forms means that the writer is a "cured" romantic.

There are five categories of romantic Lovestrokes, and each category allows for a wide range of romantic behavior. The categories are: classic romantics, long-term romantics, short-term romantics, obsessive romantics *and* nonromantics.

CLASSIC ROMANTICS

Handwriting that is schooltype in its formations, or shows a predominately schooltype influence, is produced by the classic romantic. Schooltype writers have traditional values and expectations in general, and this includes conventional romantic expectations. A schooltype writer will prefer a dramatic marriage proposal; an elaborate wedding; festive anniversary celebrations. Female schooltype writers like to be wined and dined on their dates, and male schooltype writers will willingly pick up the tab.

Here are the handwritings of an engaged couple who are both classic romantics. They are both enthusiastically anticipating their June wedding and Hawaiian honeymoon . . . and she is quite proud of her pear-shaped diamond engagement ring!

While both writings show some simplification, the forms are strongly schooltype when compared with the third writing, which shows almost no schooltype influence. The third writer is no less romantic, but she would prefer a Brazilian samba club to a Sinatra concert on a date.

This is a very exciting time in my life, full of plans & dreams. It is also a very emotional time since all of my present styles of living will have to be changed as

Hers

I love my job because I am surrounded by people with smiles all day long. The

His

Seduced, and when he asked an oracle how to produce a

Non-Schooltype-Form Writing

LONG-TERM ROMANTICS

The long-term romantic can run the gamut, from ultra-conservative to wildly conventional. The most important point is that this romantic type is capable of sustaining romantic feelings throughout the duration of a relationship. The characteristics of the long-term romantic include: emotional stability, reliability, warmth, caring and imagination. Therefore, the graphological indicators for the long-term romantic are regularity, roundedness and good spacing between lines.

- *Regularity* shows emotional stability.
- *Roundedness* shows empathy and warmth.
- *Good space between lines* shows idealism.

When I lived in New York I swore I'd live nowhere else. And then I saw it — life elsewhere It exists! But how? Differently. But that's because its elsewhere.

Long-Term Romantic

In the highly simplified handwriting of this male political analyst, we see that he has the intelligence, empathy, discipline and imagination to keep a relationship alive over a long period of time. He'll soon be celebrating his fifteenth wedding anniversary.

SHORT-TERM ROMANTICS

Short-term romantics blow hot and cold quickly. They can be madly in love one minute, totally turned off the next.

Irregularity is the hallmark of the short-term romantic. Irregularity always shows inconsistency and unpredictable behavior.

Constantly changing letter sizes and zone confusions show that this attractive female businesswoman is emotionally changeable. Her feelings toward a potential partner can change as quickly as the slant of her writing.

with advertising, merchandising + decision making. I don't know if I can take all of this. One minute loving it the next I'm in acute depression. There is some kind of an answer to all this madness. I love it I hate it.

Short-Term Romantic

OBSESSIVE ROMANTICS

Angle writers are prone to romantic obsessions. That is because the angle formation in itself requires control, and even compulsion. If you try to write an angular *M,* you will see the effort and discipline it entails—as opposed to the thread or the garland connection.

Angle writers want control in their relationships, and they tend to be more factual than feeling-oriented. But when an angle writer falls in love—after subjecting the object of his affection to many critical tests—then he will pursue a relationship with the same determination and urgency that he usually delegates to his work. Such intensity, urgency and energy translate into obsession.

ballet shoes. Betty freaks out when Jennifer tells her the news and adds that Briff is planning to take Popo

Obsessive Romantic

In the handwriting of this male reporter, angular connective forms, vertical writing (introversion) and an extremely precise, even left margin (discipline and control) co-exist with rounded forms, like the rounded lower zone loop in the *y* in the word *Betty* and the rounded lower loop of the *f* in *freaks,* the rounded upper loop in the *k* in that same word in the first line, and elsewhere throughout the writing. Therefore, we see a disciplined and organized nature that also needs love, emotional expression and release of feelings.

NONROMANTICS

Anyone who has been burned in a love affair can go through a phase of being "down on love." Some people quickly recover their natural romantic inclinations when they meet a person who interests them. For the nonromantic, love is lowest on his list of priorities—either because he is too insecure to believe that anyone could love him, or because he is more concerned with achievement and success.

The graphological indicators of the nonromantic are: upper zone emphasis, illegible middle zone, narrowness, lack of loops, angularity, wide spaces between words and lines and narrow lower zone formations.

- The *upper zone emphasis* shows intellect over emotion.
- *Illegible middle zone* shows low self-esteem.
- *Narrowness* shows inhibition and restraint.
- *Lack of loops* shows suppression of feelings and fantasies.
- *Angularity* shows tension.
- *Wide spaces between words and lines* show emotional isolation.
- *Narrow lower zone formations* show sexual inhibition.

Nonromantic

The handwriting of this male computer programmer shows all the above graphological indicators. Only an empathic, supportive, nurturing, adoring and loyal woman could inspire his romantic tendencies . . . after he allowed himself to trust her.

Now, suppose you have scrutinized a script for the romantic Lovestrokes and you still can't categorize the writer.

If you should notice a capital *D* that looks like this:

Or a small, block letter *g* that looks like this:

You're safe in concluding that the writer lives for love. Grab their hand and walk off into the sunset.

4 Sexual Lovestrokes

In the 1950s, newlyweds furtively read euphemistically titled books like Secrets of Marital Fulfillment *and* The Key to Happiness for Husband and Wife. *Naturally, "fulfillment" and "happiness" referred to a taboo subject—SEX!*

Sounds more like the Middle Ages than the middle of the twentieth century, doesn't it?

Thanks to the impact of the sexual revolution, developments in contraception, sex education in schools and the teachings of sexual media messiahs from Dr. Reuben to Dr. Ruth, sex is now an acceptable subject for dinner party conversation. Intelligent and aware adults and young adults feel entitled to a satisfying sex life. Sexuality in the eighties is considered to be a medium for emotional expression, for physical release and the relief of tension; a conduit for giving and receiving pleasure, for spiritual rejuvenation; a grown-up form of playfulness and a means of emotional bonding.

Because graphology offers insights into personality, psychological, emotional and social makeup, it naturally reveals sexual needs and drives.

A Romantic Compatibility Analysis must include a Sexual Compatibility Analysis. The Lovestrokes that show sexuality focus on physical vitality, sensuality and instinctual drives.

PHYSICAL VITALITY

Good vitality is necessary to sexual performance. Poor vitality may result in a weak libido.

Vitality is evident when the handwriting shows good energy and strong movement across the page. The following are two examples of good vitality.

There ain't nobody here at all, so quiet yourself and stop the fuss, There ain't

aquarium! the Singing toad fish of Sausalito, famous for

Good Vitality

A lack of vitality is evident when the writing moves slowly across the page, with great effort. This doesn't necessarily indicate aversion to sex, but it could be made by a writer who always "has a headache."

Robbie the Robot sold song sheets in Woolworths.

Picket-line Priscilla crawled in printwriting.

Weak Vitality

Pressure in handwriting can only be seen when the sample has been written in ballpoint pen. To determine the heaviness of the pressure, turn your handwriting sample over so that you can see the imprint of the ballpoint pen. If the pressure is good, you will be able to feel the imprint of the letters with your fingertips. If the pressure is weak, there will be hardly any imprint.

Good pressure is a sign of vitality, and, therefore, the capacity for rigorous sexual performance. Extremely heavy pressure may be a sign of either emotional or sexual aggression.

ROUNDEDNESS VERSUS ANGULARITY

In terms of one's emotional makeup, roundedness shows the tendency to be empathic, warm and expressive. As a sexual Lovestroke, rounded forms connote sensuousness. The more rounded the writing, the greater the probability that the person succumbs to pleasurable experiences.

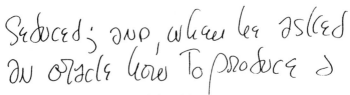

Rounded and Sensuous

Angular writing, conversely, does not necessarily connote a lack of sensuousness. But since angular forms show a need for control, the angular writer may use sex as a means for controlling others, rather than as a method of release.

Angular Writing

Let's say a twenty-two-year-old woman is simply seething with desire, but her prim body language would fool the savviest sex fiend. If her writing shows a strong schooltype influence, then she has probably been brought up to believe that "good little girls" don't enjoy sex. And, although the forms may be sensuously rounded, if the loops and letters are narrow, then inhibition may triumph over lustful desires.

The narrowness of the letters in the angular writing shown above tell us that the writer is inhibited.

A sexually uninhibited writing would show rounded forms (sensuousness), wide letters (lack of inhibition, strong emotions), a narrow right margin (pursuit of intimacy) and energetic movement (energy and vitality).

Sensuous and Sexually Uninhibited

SLANT

Slant must be taken into consideration when looking at sexual Love-strokes. You might assume that a right slant writer might be more willing to please a sexual partner than a self-contained vertical writer. But sexuality is the most private, multifaceted expression of our unconscious impulses. Some vertical writers may achieve their greatest release through sexual activity. In the writing below, the vertical writing is combined with fluid movement, rounded forms and large lower loops.

nothing else seems important ... the thing that matters is that you are

Upright But Sensuous

When the handwriting sample descends to the very bottom of the page, there is interest in eroticism. In this respect, the lower margin is similar to the lower zone—the zone expressing unconscious impulses and sexual desires. A handwriting with a narrow lower margin indicates that the writer is not fearful of the dictates of the unconscious, including sexuality. However, a wide lower margin might show sexual reticence or fear of sex.

But the single most important factor in sexual Lovestrokes is the lower zone. This zone clearly depicts the writer's interest in sex, need for sex, level of sexual fulfillment and frequency of sexual fantasies.

THE LOWER ZONE AND THE BASE LINE

According to graphologist Roger Rubin, lower loop formations may have a different significance in male and female writings.

The lower zone is the zone of the unconscious, and thus of hidden emotional needs. Therefore, says Rubin, "because of their socialization, many men, unlike many women, have difficulties with their emotional expression . . . and sex becomes the one arena where it is legitimate for them to contact their deeper feeling states and to express them. So the sex act carries the burden of emotional expression. This may partly explain the urgency with which so many men approach sex."

In other words, if indicators showing emotional repression are present in a male handwriting, but there is a strong lower zone emphasis, it can show that the writer releases his pent-up feelings through the sex act.

Emotional Inhibition/Sexual Fantasy

Generally speaking, when there is interest in sex, there are formations in the lower zone.

Not all these formations need be loops. In highly simplified writings, a preference for straight lines can be a function of simplification.

Lower Zone Simplification

Most handwritings, however, will show loops in the lower zone.

Ideally, a loop that is rounded and closes at the base line symbolizes sexual fulfillment.

Let's use the letter *y* to demonstrate the varieties of lower loop formations.

The base line represents your conscious mind. Loops that close at the base line show that the writer has no barriers between the conscious mind (base line) and unconscious impulses (lower zone formations). Graphologist Felix Klein asserts that "the proper crossing point for the realization of instinctual drives is the base line. If the loop is closed above or below the base line, it means that the instinctual needs are suppressed—and probably sublimated or transferred into different areas."

For example, in the handwriting below, the writer's high degree of emotional tension, seen in the excessive angularity, has caused him to sublimate his sexual and emotional impulses into career ambitions seen in the overemphasized upper zone.

I'm not thinking about it

Sexual Sublimation

Let's look at the many possibilities for lower zone formations. Your handwriting may contain one—or a combination—of these Lovestrokes.

Short loop
This shows an avoidance of sex, or lack of interest in sex.

Wide loop
Sexual interest, but frustration.

Extremely wide loop
Obsessive sexual interest, great frustration and many unfulfilled sexual fantasies.

Unclosed loops
In a woman's script, a possible inability to have an orgasm. In a man's script, unfulfilled sexual fantasies and a search for satisfaction.

Angular loops
Aggression that could manifest sexually.

Long lower loops
Interest in sex.

Long lower loops that don't return to base line
Interest in sex, but lack of fulfillment or repression.

Peculiar loops
Sexual kinkiness.

Varying lower loops
Sexual unpredictability; hedonism; desire for erotic experimentation.

Narrow loops
Sexual shyness, self-consciousness and inhibition.

Drifting left loops
In men, sexuality as a tool for receiving "mothering."

Lower loops that descend into upper zone of next line
Sexual fantasies; possible lack of control over sexual impulses.

Loops that close in the middle zone
In men, sexual shyness. In women, self-consciousness about being overweight; sensitivity to touch or "girlishness."

SEXUAL COMPATIBILITY CHECKLIST

What are your requirements in a lover?

Do you have a strong sex drive, and therefore you need a mate who will want frequent sex?
Then look for good vitality (energy and pressure), roundedness (sensuousness) and rounded lower loops that close at the base line (sexual fulfillment).

Are you erotically experimental?
Then look for an unconventional handwriting (simplified, creative forms), variety in lower zone formations (experimentation), wide letters and widening left margin (lack of inhibition), narrow lower margin (erotic interests) and lower zone loops descending into the upper zone of the next line (sexual fantasies).

Men: Do you insist that the ladies you bed be orgasmic?
Then look for rounded forms, good pressure, and rounded lower loops that close at the base line (sexual fulfillment).

Are you worried that he might be promiscuous?
A handwriting with an overemphasis on lower loops (sexual obsession), combined with a thread connective form (willingness to give into impulses), widening left margin (spontaneity triumphs over self-control), narrow right margin (ease at intimacy), could mean that he chooses sexual conquest over self-control.

Is she straight? Is he gay?
Since stereotypes about masculinity and femininity are no longer applied to contemporary gay and lesbian behavior, it is difficult to see sexual identity in handwriting . . . but you can see if they are sexually passionate.

Does he have sexual hang-ups?
Extreme loops in the lower zone show conflicts, anxieties and problems regarding sex.

(continued)

(continued)

Women: Are you looking to avoid Mr. Goodbar?

Then stay away from a writer whose script shows extremely heavy pressure (anger), angles in the lower zone (sexual aggression), angular formations (tension) and any extremes (problems).

Do you like hugging and cuddling as much as sex?

Roundedness; right slant; narrow, even spaces between words; balanced lower zone loops all show a desire to please and emotional warmth.

Do you wonder why he rarely initiates lovemaking?

Narrow loops may show inhibition.

Short loops, weak pressure may show low libido, lack of interest in sex.

Middle zone or upper zone emphasis, with avoidance of the lower zone, shows fear of sex, or sex as lowest priority.

Are you seeking someone who is more cerebral than sensual, more religious than randy, more spiritual than sexy?

Look for a writing with an upper zone emphasis, and a minimal lower zone.

Sexual preferences are highly individualized. Some lovers like to be sexual "teacher"—and so they search for someone less experienced than themselves. Many women prefer a man who has had a great deal of sexual experience. There are people who want to dominate their mates—and just as many who want to be dominated. For certain folks, sex should be playful and fun, while others take their lovemaking very seriously.

Let's see how these characteristics are manifested through the Sexual Lovestrokes Analysis.

Strong right slant, lots of loops, long lower loops that cross at the base line—this twenty-seven-year-old chiropractor is sensuous, sexually oriented, emotional and tender, and aims to please his partner.

because they feel good for a change. That makes everyone involved happy.

Narrowness of letters, general angularity, angles in the lower zone show that sex is a source of tension and a means of control for this thirty-six-year-old woman who is a dominatrix.

the very walls speak of it without any embarrasment — maybe they've been here too long ... Do you think ?/

Good pressure, vitality, rounded lower loops, but the schooltype quality of this writing hints that this forty-year-old man is certainly sexy, but too conservative to be the ideal candidate for acting out outrageous fantasies.

I rarely fry eggs on a griddle, certainly not every day. Likely the only thing that

Acting out erotic fantasies might appeal to this thirty-five-year-old salesman whose handwriting shows creative forms (imagination), simplification and varying lower loops (eroticism, hedonism).

To Italy and France, also Turkey and Hungary?

The high degree of control, even rigidity, the conventional school-type forms (strict upbringing), the extremely wide spaces between words (emotional isolation) and narrow letters (shyness), combined with narrow lower loops (inhibition), would almost inevitably be present in the writing of this twenty-nine-year-old female virgin.

Well maybe not 12 - but you get the picture. Thank God these are all interesting and successful women in

Rounded forms here co-exist with extremely round loops in the lower zone in the handwriting of this thirty-two-year-old pregnant woman. In this case, the extreme forms may be a symbolic picture of the woman's feelings about her body during pregnancy.

This pregnancy has been difficult on my body and I really can't wait until this baby is born. I've been

Strong rightward movement, incredible vitality, wide letters and roundedness, with long lower loops that close at the base line, tell you that this forty-five-year-old woman is sensuous, sexy and uninhibited sexually!

Keeping people awake at night with their sexual humming, had moved in!

Rounded forms and full lower loops that close at the base line are combined with strong simplification. This thirty-two-year-old man embodies the best elements of intelligence and sensuality.

It could be that it wasn't that far away to begin with. You don't know that until you leave. And then, its Too Late!

A lack of loops in the lower zone, combined with strong simplification and an upper zone emphasis, indicates that this thirty-seven-year-old man is more intellectual than sexually oriented, but the strong right slant also shows the desire to please a partner—and that includes the sexual arena.

Nixon had enemies and we all knew we were "on the list." Reagon can do something awful but he

5 Compromisability

Being single allows you to be selfish. You can eat whatever and whenever you want, establish your own bedtimes, vacation where you please.

You don't have to worry about his chronic insomnia, or her high-protein diet, or his fondness for blasting the stereo, or her mother's telephone calls.

Yet most people would gladly eventually trade in their autonomy for matrimony . . . or a live-in lover.

The moment you take your wedding vows, decide to live together or suddenly feel "serious" about somebody, the challenge of compromise begins. You must consider—and cope with—your partner's needs, moods, tastes, habits and even biological rhythms.

There will be times when your two great minds will think alike. After all, similar sensibilities attracted you in the first place.

But, sooner or later, you will be forced to confront a sticky situation.

It may be a simple dispute over whether your daughter should attend ballet school. Or it may be an emotionally charged in-law issue. A wife may feel that her privacy is violated when her sister-in-law drops over without calling first. Her husband insists, "When it comes to my baby sister, the door to my home is always open!"

Sometimes maintaining a strong stance is important to the health of the relationship. Sometimes working out a creative solution is best. Then, there are times when self-sacrifice is called for.

Not every compromise agreement is irrevocable. Compromise agreements can be amended, reversed or expanded. Consider the couple who believed in traditional male and female roles when they married years ago. They agreed that she would do the housework, and he'd be responsible for mowing the lawn, washing the car and cleaning the garage. When she took on a demanding job, he grudgingly offered to wash the dinner dishes. Today, she is *head of her department, takes frequent business trips and shares housework responsibilities almost equally with her husband.*

During the dynamic and unpredictable course of a relationship, the interests and attitudes, demands and priorities, of each partner may change. Boyfriend and girlfriend, husband and wife, will be tested to accept new situations.

So when you're considering making a commitment to a relationship, you might want to look at the Lovestrokes that rate compromisability.

The components of compromisability are: emotional flexibility versus emotional control, selflessness, self-interest and selfishness.

EMOTIONAL FLEXIBILITY

Like a weeping willow tree, the emotionally flexible writer will bend with the wind. This writer accommodates easily to meet the other person's needs or to benefit the relationship. The emotionally flexible writer has less interest in always being "right" than in working through problems for mutual satisfaction.

For instance, Harry wanted to go wind-surfing in the Caribbean for his vacation. His wife, Joan, had her heart set on a camping trip in Wyoming. Cognizant of the fact that Joan had recently been under emotional stress because her mother was undergoing chemotherapy treatments for cancer, Harry agreed to go camping. He realized that Joan's happiness was a bigger concern than his pleasure.

GARLAND CONNECTION

The foremost indicator of emotional flexibility is the garland connection. This is seen in handwritings where the small *m*'s, *n*'s and *h*'s have an angle on the top and a bow on the bottom. This formation reveals a good-natured and adaptable disposition, an abhorrence of conflict, the capacity to enjoy life and the desire to avoid stress.

Here is the garland connection.

The following is an example of the garland connection as seen in the handwriting of a fifty-three-year-old male. Here garland connections co-exist with an expanding left margin—a possible indication of lavishness and enthusiasm. His garlands are in keeping with his joie de vivre. Orig-

love, sex & survival in the eighties. I'm sure your book will be instrumental in helping many people to a fuller realization of

Flexible

inal forms show thoughtfulness and creativity . . . and wide, even spaces between words and lines tell you that he has the good judgment necessary to sustain a successful, unstressful relationship, including the willingness to compromise when necessary.

THREAD CONNECTION

The thread connection is seen in handwritings when the small *m*'s, *n*'s and *h*'s are abbreviated. This formation is made by the writer who has learned how to "maneuver" through life by use of charm and intuition; who is capable of seeing all sides of any story, and who therefore can switch a stance without much emotional strain. When a thread writer makes a compromise, it's usually because he can accommodate the other person's viewpoint.

Here are examples of some of the many possibilities for the thread connection.

Here is an example of the thread connection in a handwriting.

wrongly suggesting a person whose sense of career led him to seek haven in an exiting institution. The point

Accommodating

In the handwriting of this forty-year-old male, thread connections co-exist with an extreme right slant . . . and, thus, a desire to please others and make contact with them, a willingness to compromise.

LACK OF RESTRAINT

Lack of restraint is seen in a handwriting that flows spontaneously and impulsively across the page. The unrestrained writer lives by his own rules, and so, when it comes to compromise, he can readily change those rules to gratify his partner.

Here is an example of a handwriting that shows a lack of restraint.

It's a wonderful feeling to just let go of the stress of daily life and just slide back into/onto the soft mattress of your imag-

Unrestrained and Accommodating

In the handwriting of this thirty-five-year-old male, wide letter formations (emotionalism, lack of inhibition) are present in script that moves freely and energetically across the page. This writing is so free in comparison to the schooltype model that we can judge the thread connections as being the hallmark of a bona fide nonconformist. The "looseness," or lack of rigidity, shows that he has no compunction to maintain a strong stance—so he will readily compromise.

None of the above graphological indicators guarantee that the writer will always have high compromisability in a relationship. They do, however, suggest that the writer will be less resistant to compromise than the emotionally controlled writer.

EMOTIONAL CONTROL

The controlled partner will refuse to compromise, will compromise reluctantly or will compromise after determining that a change of heart would be self-beneficial or necessary to the maintenance of the relationship.

For instance, Angela was the oldest of five children. When she was ten years old, her father abandoned her alcoholic mother. Organized and intelligent, Angela held the family together, while her mother habitually passed out on the living-room couch.

When she married Stan, a gentle and modest computer programmer, Angela was accustomed to being the boss. Her younger siblings had never questioned her authority. During the first few years of marriage, Stan was amenable to playing by Angela's rules. But when he got a major promotion, he became more confident—and more assertive. When Angela sensed that continued rigidity would threaten her marriage, she began to compromise.

ANGLE CONNECTION

The primary graphological indicator for emotional control is the angle connection. This is seen in handwritings when the small *m*'s, *n*'s and *h*'s are angular on top and bottom. This formation is made by the writer who is naturally predisposed to conflict; who wishes to impose his will onto others; who thinks he knows what is best for others, and who perceives inflexibility as an asset. On the positive side, the angle connection shows discipline, strong willpower and the capacity for efficiency.

Here is the angle connection.

Here is an example of the angle connection as seen in a handwriting.

Controlled and Intellectual

In this handwriting of a thirty-three-year-old male, angle connections are combined with extreme simplification of form, so simplified that it is practically printed. Such simplification connotes a superior intellect. This writer's angles reflect his precision and exacting standards. He will compromise if he finds his partner's arguments intellectually acceptable.

ANGULAR FORMS

Angular forms are seen when sharp, straight lines appear in the place of loops. Angular forms can be seen in any zone.

Here is an example of a handwriting containing angular forms.

Uncompromising and Angry

In this handwriting of a thirty-six-year-old female, angular forms are seen in the absence of loops in all zones. Angles are also made through letter formations and connections—the piercing upper zone formation of the *h* in *the* in the first line, the angular tops of the small *s*'s and the *p* in *steps* in that line, the upper zone angle of the *b* in *buns* in that line . . . and elsewhere throughout the handwriting. Such excessive angularity is a sign of inner tension, anger and the tendency to control one's emotions rather than spontaneously surrendering to one's feelings. Naturally, given this propensity, such a writer will resist compromise, as it entails submitting to the demands of another person.

ARCADE CONNECTIONS

Arcade connections can indicate emotional control. Arcades are seen in handwritings where the small *m*'s, *n*'s and *h*'s have a bow on the top and an angle on the bottom. The formation is made by writers who suppress emotional expression to maintain social propriety. Their parents taught them to always do the "proper" thing. Because of this, the arcade writer is less spontaneous than the garland or thread writer . . . and less amenable to compromise.

Here is the arcade connection.

Here is an example of the arcade connection as seen in a handwriting.

Overcontrolled

In the handwriting of this thirty-two-year-old female, arcade connections co-exist with vertical writing, rigidity of forms, extreme regularity and extremely wide spaces between words. Because her upbringing emphasized being a "good" rather than a "happy" girl, she learned to maintain social poise at all costs. Now, she exerts so much control over her emotions that she has become inflexible.

SELFLESSNESS

The selfless writer places his partner's needs above his own. Pleasing others is his main priority. When it comes to compromise, the selfless writer can be depended upon to accommodate. This is both positive and negative. While initially the pleasure of having one's own way can be gratifying, the relationship can also become boring, unchallenging and one-sided. A strong-willed partner who once thrived on being dominant may grow to desire equality.

For instance, as the seventh child of nine, Charlie was starved for attention in his chaotic household. He discovered that doing his older siblings' chores for them got him approval and attention. When he moved in with Roberta, a vivacious free-lance photographer, he devoted himself to pleasing her. Roberta proudly told her feminist friends, "Charlie not only cooks dinner, but he does the dishes afterwards, too!" When decisions had to be made, Roberta made them. The relationship ended when Roberta became less politically dogmatic and more desirous of a "quality" relationship. She left Charlie for an opinionated, charismatic filmmaker she "respected."

Unless your mate is a modern-day Gandhi, the impulse toward selflessness is probably an extension of emotional dependency and low self-esteem. This writer compromises to sustain the relationship at any cost.

The graphological indicators for emotional dependency are: extreme right slant, narrow spaces between words, narrow right margin and left-drifting lower loops. The middle zone may also be unformed or illegible.

- *Extreme right slant* shows dependency and a need to please.
- *Narrow spaces between words* show the need for social contact.
- *Narrow right margins* show other-orientation.
- *Left-drifting lower loops* show a need for mothering.
- *An illegible or unformed middle zone* shows low self-esteem.

Here is an example of a handwriting that includes all these indicators.

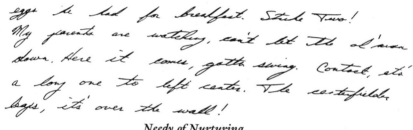

Needy of Nurturing

In the handwriting of this twenty-eight-year-old male, the extreme right slant shows a need to reach out to others, but extremely narrow letters and extremely wide spaces between words show shyness. The left-drifting lower loops imply the need for mothering, thus the willingness to compromise based on a need to please, a desire to be nurtured and a lack of assertiveness due to shyness.

SELF-INTEREST

A partner with a healthy self-interest will compromise to please his or her mate or to benefit the relationship, but not at the cost of self-destructiveness. For instance, Elizabeth was ambivalent about leaving her two-year-old daughter to return to her college-teaching job. As soon as she entered the classroom, Elizabeth realized how intellectually deprived she had felt staying home with her child, despite the emotional rewards mothering conferred. With the help of a babysitter, she managed to successfully juggle being a professor and a parent. Elizabeth was up for tenure when her daughter turned three. Her husband, whose older brother was twelve when he was born, began campaigning to have a second child, convinced that "siblings should be close in age." Elizabeth heeded his persuasive arguments, and then worked out a compromise that was mutually beneficial—she would wait to get tenure, and get pregnant during a sabbatical the subsequent year. That way, she would insure her job security, plan a five-year age difference between her children, and make her husband happy.

The graphological indicators for self-interest are the indicators of high self-esteem. They include: regularity, legibility and a well-defined middle zone.

- *Regularity* shows emotional stability.
- *Legibility* shows clarity about oneself.
- A *well-defined middle zone* shows ego strength.

Here is an example of a handwriting that includes all these indicators.

Healthy Self-Interest

In the handwriting of this thirty-one-year-old female, regularity, legibility and a well-defined middle zone all show high self-esteem. Extreme simplification and creative forms, combined with wide, even spaces between words, show a high intellect and excellent social judgment. This writer is smart enough to know when compromise is called for—and secure enough to avoid jeopardizing her own security.

SELF-CENTEREDNESS

Self-centered partners have difficulty with compromise, either because they were spoiled as children, or because they were deprived. These writers see to it that their needs and whims get met.

For instance, Myra was the only child of older parents who had wanted to start a family for years. They doted on her as if they were grandparents. Every night, her father brought her a present when he came home from work.

After graduating from college, Myra moved back home. Her parents didn't charge her for room or board, so Myra spent her secretary's salary on clothing, jewelry and cosmetics. When she got married, Myra expected her husband, Stan, to support her in style. When Stan's paycheck was cut, he asked Myra to cancel her country club membership. Infuriated, Myra stormed back to her parents' house . . . and stayed there until Stan capitulated.

The graphological indicators for self-centeredness are: an overemphasized middle zone; overly large capitals and returning left endstrokes.

- The *overemphasized middle zone* shows excessive self-concern.
- *Overly large capitals* show obsession with the impression one makes on others and one's own appearance.
- *Returning left endstrokes* show a return to the self.

Here is an example of returning left endstrokes.

Here is an example of overly large capitals.

Here is an example of a handwriting that includes these indicators.

Self-centeredness

The handwriting of this thirty-three-year-old female is characterized by huge letter formations; an overly large middle zone; and returning left endstrokes. In a relationship, her preoccupation with fulfilling her own needs would inhibit compromise.

Those are the Lovestrokes that measure compromisability. Remember that every relationship presents its own sets of challenges and demands. It is impossible to predict how a person will react in a specific situation, but you can draw some general conclusions about the compromisability potential between any two writers. And, of course, anyone who wants to make a relationship work can learn the fine art of compromise.

COMPROMISING PAIRINGS

If a garland writer gets together with an angle writer, the former will probably end up doing more compromising than the latter.

A garland writer and a thread writer could reach compromises, but the latter may manipulate the former into accepting a new stance.

An unrestrained writer will probably encourage a restrained writer to become more flexible—and to compromise.

An arcade writer may challenge an angle writer to compromise.

A regular writer may loosen up around an irregular writer—and compromise.

A selfless writer will be eager to compromise with a self-centered writer.

A self-interest writer will eventually refuse to compromise with a self-centered writer.

Two self-interest writers will show the good judgment, strength of character and maturity to work out mutually beneficial compromises.

---

6 Evaluating Your Values: Materialism versus Spiritualism

Good communication and good sex are important aspects of romantic relationships.

But evaluating romantic compatibility also requires evaluating values.

Let's say that one partner likes to play the stock market . . . and the other wants to donate her life savings to charity.

Let's say one partner is a born-again Christian . . . and the other is a fervent Marxist.

Let's say one partner spends Sundays at the local library . . . and the other at the shopping mall.

Will these contrasting values be a source of stimulation . . . or a guarantee of irritation?

A Lovestrokes Analysis can show you whether a writer's value system is oriented toward the material, the spiritual or the philosophical.

Let's start by looking at the Lovestrokes that reveal materialism, or attitudes toward money.

MATERIALISM

Sigmund Freud said that sex and money come from the same source. By this remark, he meant that money can provide a sense of power that is similar to the feeling of sexual potency. The drive to make money may be a sublimation of the sex drive.

Rhode Island graphologist Marc Seifer has noted that the scripts of high-powered salesmen often show sexual frustration.

For this reason, lower zone loops can symbolize monetary interests as well as sexual desires.

When money is used as a substitute for sex, we see a handwriting that is frequently schooltype in form, with a strongly emphasized or legible middle zone, an underemphasized upper zone and extreme lower loops.

The schooltype form shows adherence to conventional values—and the standard American Dream is getting rich.

The middle zone emphasis shows realism and practicality rather than idealism or spirituality.

And the extreme lower loops indicate sexual frustrations.

So the writer overcomes the frustration by making money—instead of making love.

Here is an example of a handwriting that contains all these indicators. This forty-year-old male lawyer puts in regular eighty-hour workweeks so that he can retire in luxury at age forty-five. Heavy pressure here also shows aggression and strong willpower. Note how all the upper zone letter formations are pushed into the middle zone.

Strong Material Drives

Materialism is also seen whenever there is a disproportionate middle zone. Since the middle zone is the zone that represents tangible, concrete things, routines and daily functioning, it shows material concerns, since money is such an important part of daily life.

Here is an example of a disproportionate middle zone in the handwriting of a twenty-two-year-old female songwriter who is attempting to overcome her upbringing by parents who wanted her to "marry for money."

Materialistic

A third indicator of materialism is the garland connection, seen in handwritings where the small *m*'s, *n*'s and *h*'s show an angle at the top and a bow at the bottom.

Here is an example of the garland connection.

Writers who employ the garland connection are pleasure- and comfort-oriented. They abhor conflict and wish that everyone were as easygoing and flexible as they are. They also crave ease in living, and have a fondness for material comforts and luxury. Garland writers have champagne tastes and enjoy traveling first class. But because they're so easygoing, they don't want to exert themselves to obtain the finer things in life. They would rather be supported by someone, or they might live on credit and loans.

Here is an example of a handwriting containing garland connections. It belongs to a waitress who works three days a week. An amateur clothing designer, she buys her seasonal wardrobes during her bi-yearly jaunts to Europe.

Luxury-Loving

After you have determined the writer's interest in monetary matters, you might want to know how he, or she, handles their finances.

Does he sock it all away in a Swiss bank account? Does she spend her last dime on her wardrobe? Is he secretly a Scrooge? Is she a closet philanthropist?

GENEROSITY

A generous nature is seen in a handwriting that contains wide letters, roundedness and a strong movement to the right. These indicators show a lack of restraint and a desire to please others.

The following is a handwriting that contains all these indicators. This thirty-four-year-old male art dealer serves caviar instead of cold cuts at his gallery opening parties.

Generous

When the above indicators are combined with a widening left margin—lavishness, impulsiveness, haste—the writer may be generous to the point of extravagance.

Opposite is an example of an extravagant handwriting. This thirty-eight-year-old male radio talk show host is capable of indulging both himself and the people he entertains. Note the wide letter formations, wide letters and strong movement to the right.

A connoisseur—a person who only buys the best and wants value for his dollar—will have wide, even left and right margins.

Opposite is an example of a connoisseur, in the handwriting of a thirty-five-year-old male record industry executive and painter who also collects antiques. The refined aesthetic sensibilities are also seen in the beautiful, almost calligraphic letter formations.

Thriftiness is seen in a tight, narrow, controlled handwriting on the facing page. In the handwriting of this twenty-eight-year-old male photographer, excessive rigidity and control indicate tightness over emotions—and probably over finances, too.

SPIRITUALITY

Suppose you meet a woman at a party and she invites you over for dinner the following Friday. The meal consists of marinated tofu, grated cabbage salad and millet patties. As she serves you, your new lady love gives an impassioned speech about the ecological practicality of the vegetarian diet. Driving home, you wonder, "Is she sincere . . . or a flake?"

The handwriting of a person whose nature is genuinely idealistic would have good legibility—showing integrity—lack of zone confusion—showing clarity of values—and high extensions in the upper zone—showing idealistic inclinations.

Opposite is an example of an idealistic handwriting, from a thirty-

outloud. Fascinated by the special place — the mental state — I would visit, I could amuse myself endlessly.

Extravagance

also begun a class in italic calligraphy where I discovered alternate "tails" and letter-couplings, as well as some attractive capitals that I was eager to incorporate into my handwriting. I adopted these two influences to begin creating a hybrid style of my own. Along the way, I would notice interesting capitals or various other attractive elements in the handwriting of others. After years of borrowings and casting-off, I settled into my current style. All told, the process took about a decade of deliberate fine-tuning.

Connoisseur

In a room where lovers go talking on the telephone. But ATT put an end to that. Now what will the lovers do. They can't smoke —

Thrifty

Whenever Satsuma gets a present, she saves it for her momma. When her momma gets a present, she gives it to her momma, Mrs. Aelia Lee Snow. Satsuma gave her momma some pink

Spirituality and Idealism

eight-year-old female poet who does volunteer work teaching poetry writing to prison inmates.

Let's try another scenario. Girl meets boy, invites him over for dinner. He arrives with a bottle of *Beaujolais nouveau,* and she quickly confesses that she forgot to put the roast in the oven because she got carried away writing a poem. Is she the Emily Dickinson of the eighties . . . or a flake?

If a handwriting is extremely creative, with strong simplification, then you can conclude that the writer's main priority is self-expression. In the handwriting of this thirty-five-year-old female novelist and professor, thread connections show nonconformity, and a lack of middle zone emphasis with a highly extended upper zone reveal that material considerations are secondary to creative self-expression.

Self-Expressive, Nonmaterialistic

But interest in self-expression does not necessitate disdain for the material world. If the handwriting contains good simplification, creative forms, a legible, pronounced middle zone and garlands, the writer may thrive on self-expression—but you won't catch them toiling away in a garret.

Here is an example of a handwriting that reveals self-expression and materialism.

This thirty-four-year-old ballerina collects rare oriental rugs.

Self-Expressive and Materialistic

Those are the Lovestrokes that tell us about the writer's value system.

When determining the romantic compatibility potential, similarity in values may enhance your rapport. Contrasting values may work symbiotically. If both partners are obsessed with making millions, they may spend all their time trading commodities and forget to trade terms of endearment. This may suit them fine—or eventually lead to estrangement.

If both partners are idealistic, they might donate so much money to preventing world hunger that they need to borrow from friends to pay the rent! This might be mutually amusing or eventually prove annoying!

Consider the old adage that "opposites attract."

If she's a comfort-loving garland writer who is writing the Great American Novel, and he's a Wall Street Whiz Kid . . . then he can be her lover and her patron.

If he's a struggling painter who uses packing crates for chairs and forgets to eat for days at a time, and she's a registered nurse who changes her sheets twice weekly and fixes three squares a day, she can pose for his paintings . . . and monitor his calorie intake!

7 Commitment: The Relationship Issue of the Eighties

"Commitment" is one of the most often employed "buzzwords" of the eighties. Magazine articles, television talk shows, radio programs focus on one's ability—or inability—to make a commitment to a relationship.

Three decades ago, when divorce was the rare exception and not the rule, commitment wasn't even an issue.

But consider how times have changed.

In most urban areas, single, available women greatly outnumber single, available men. With so many opportunities to date, why should a man "tie himself down" with one woman?

Women today are competing with men in every profession. Women no longer depend on men for financial support. Advances in medicine enable them to safely postpone childbirth into their forties, or to become artificially inseminated. Single parenthood has gained in acceptance. If a woman doesn't "need" a man for his money or as a parental presence, why should she tie herself down? Relationships require a lot of work, and the demands of a career are hard enough.

But despite the options available to us, and in the face of the glamorous lures of the single life, most people do eventually make a commitment. They make a commitment because they find partnership preferable to solitude, and because they want to have children within the context of a nuclear family.

Yet, eighties lovers are aware that divorce is an easily available option. Making a commitment to a relationship or marriage means having the resolve to stick it out when others may choose to simply "get out."

Before getting married, living together or starting a family, a wise couple might compare their attitudes toward commitment.

They could begin by asking what "commitment" really means.

According to Dr. Robert Sternberg, it consists of "both a short-term decision to love another person and a long-term commitment to maintain that love."

Graphologist Roger Rubin defines commitment this way:

> Commitment is the desire or capacity to share one's feelings, activities and resources with another in a steady, ongoing manner. It requires a willingness to work at maintaining and improving your involvement.
>
> Commitment is expending yourself for the sake of a relationship, making a sustained effort to work through and around obstacles. Commitment means accepting the responsibility for caring, putting yourself on the line even when it's easier and less painful to withdraw.

When making a commitment, both partners must realize that real marriages do not thrive "happily ever after." People grow and change at different rates. The most intimate, loving relationships will have rocky periods and times of distance and alienation. A mature commitment means a commitment to confront these inevitable problems while enjoying the rewards of intimacy.

Graphology cannot predict whether someone will make a commitment to you—that depends on them! It can, however, answer the following questions:

- Will it be a mature commitment that reflects a desire for exclusivity, an ability to focus on another person, the acceptance of the concept of mutual growth and the maturity to organize one's life around the needs of the relationship?

- Will it be an immature commitment, reflecting the unconscious belief that all the work necessitated in a relationship will be done automatically? Is it a commitment that abdicates emotional responsibility?

- Or is this person so neurotic and disturbed that he is truly incapable of making a long-term commitment?

Let's discuss the graphological indicators of the handwriting of the mature committer.

MATURE COMMITMENT

A mature person would have a good sense of self, a developed value system and a strong sense of reality. Therefore, the Lovestrokes showing the ability to make a mature commitment would be: zone clarity and definition; lack of zone confusion; a well-formed middle zone and round-edness.

- *Clarity and lack of zone confusion* show well-defined values and maturity.
- *A well-defined middle zone* shows high self-esteem.
- *Roundedness* shows a capacity for empathy with a mate.

Here is an example of handwriting by a happily married man:

and I had grown embarassed of it. Concurrently, I had also begun a class in italic calligraphy where I discovered alternate "tails" and letter-couplings, as well as some attractive capitals that I was eager to incorporate into my handwriting. I adopted these two influences to begin creating

Mature Commitment

The beautifully developed forms in this handwriting show personal and intellectual development. Clarity and lack of zone interference show a well-defined value system and strong sense of self. Although the connective form is angular, the writing is rounded, so that the angularity can be interpreted as a sign of good discipline. Neat margins and general clarity also show a strong sense of responsibility, crucial to a mature commitment.

Here is the handwriting of a happily cohabiting woman:

Whenever Satiuma gets a present, she saves it for her momma. When her momma gets a present, she gives it to her momma, Mrs. Delia Lee Snow. Satiuma gave her momma some pink

Mature Commitment

The clear, simplified forms of this handwriting also indicate good personal development and a strong sense of self. Fine balance between the three zones shows security in one's values—she has made a commitment because she knows what she wants. Good organization and straight margins show discipline and responsibility, also necessary to a successful relationship. Though strongly vertical, the writing is highly rounded, showing a sensitivity to the needs of her partner.

SENTIMENTAL COMMITMENT

When a handwriting shows a strong schooltype influence, indicating conventional values, coupled with extreme narrowness of the space between the lines, showing a sentimental nature, we can conclude that the writer will make a sentimental commitment. In other words, she enters into a marriage because she feels that she is supposed to if she is to be societally acceptable and because marriage fulfills her sentimental fantasies of bridal showers, honeymoons, anniversaries and photograph albums filled with pictures of all of the above.

Here is an example from an engaged woman:

My boyfriend's name is Danny. He is 6'3", light skinned, blond and very generous. Right now he's working for Random House publishers, which he likes very much.

Sentimental Commitment

In this handwriting sample, we see schooltype letter formations and narrow spaces between lines, showing that this engaged young woman has conventional values and a sentimental nature.

DEPENDENT COMMITMENT

Whenever an extreme right slant is present in a handwriting, we can conclude that the writer has an emotionally dependent nature. If left-drifting lower loops are seen in a man's handwriting, it shows that dependency needs arise out of a desire for unconditional "mothering" by a mate. Clarity and regularity show the capacity to make a stable and enduring commitment.

Please come in late July because my garden will be in full bloom, and the weather

Dependent Commitment

In the handwriting of this gay man, extreme right slant and left-drifting lower loops show a strong desire to please and to be needed, coupled with an equally strong need to be "mothered" by his partner.

INCAPABLE OF COMMITMENT

Finally, let's examine the category of people who are virtually incapable of making a commitment. They may marry, but their marriages are doomed to failure. They may date, but eventually they will sabotage the relationship. People who are incapable of commitment are invariably reacting to childhood trauma, negative adult experiences, severe immaturity and a tendency toward the bizarre.

The Lovestrokes of a person incapable of commitment would be: an extreme left margin; extreme irregularity; an extreme right margin; abundant, odd letter formations; poorly organized space; neglected forms and a disturbed lower zone.

- *Extreme left margin* shows that the writer is running away from the past.
- *Extreme irregularity* shows erratic behavior.
- *Extreme right margin* shows a fear of the responsibilities and demands of the future.
- *Odd letter formations* show abnormal character structure.
- *Poorly organized space* shows poor judgment and emotional confusion.
- *Neglected forms* show a lack of discipline.
- *A disturbed lower zone* may show sexual identity conflicts.

The following are two examples of young men who recently broke off short-term relationships.

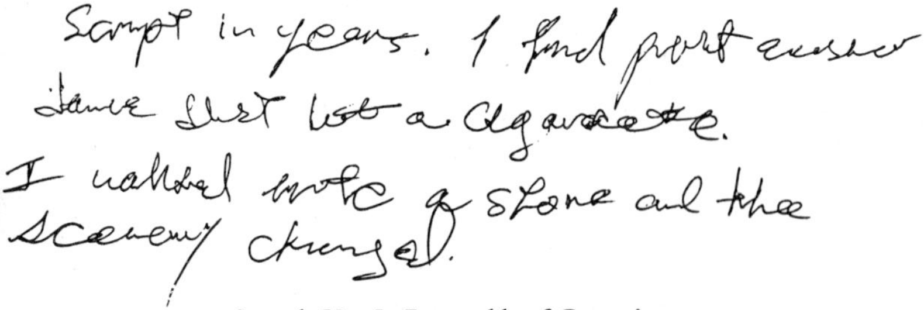

[Handwritten text at top of page, partially illegible:]

Script in years. I find first never
dance first but a cigarette.
I walked into a stone and the
scenery changed.

Sample No. 1: Incapable of Commitment

This extremely handsome young man was a physically abused child—and his handwriting shows the scars. Total neglect of the middle zone and the bizarre capital *I* formation in the first line show irreparable ego damage. This handwriting is totally erratic, utterly illegible, and filled with bizarre forms: the *f* in *find* in the first line, the two *t*'s in *cigarette* in the second line, the lower loop of the *g* in *changed* in the last line—almost every letter is disturbed. He may seduce women with his good looks, but he is too confused to make commitments to them.

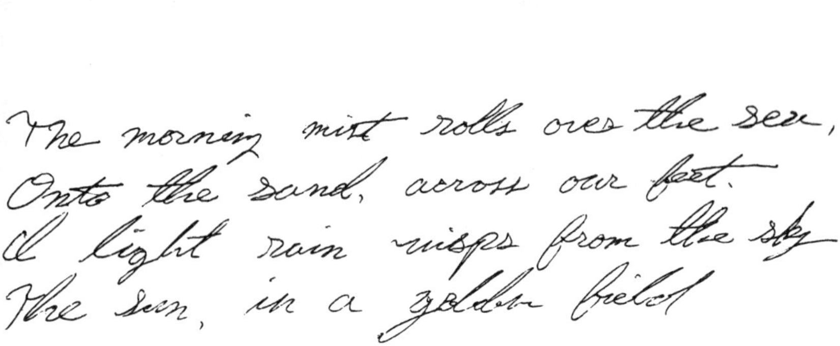

[Handwritten text:]

The morning mist rolls over the sea,
Onto the sand, across our feet.
A light rain wisps from the sky
The sun, in a golden field

Sample No. 2: Incapable of Commitment

In sample number 2, the writing of a twenty-two-year-old sexual aids salesman, we see extremely disturbed forms. The writing is illegible and filled with "knots"—like the twisted *o* in the word *golden* in the fourth line. The extreme right slant (emotional dependency) is contradicted by extremely wide spaces between words. Lower loops drifting to the left show a need for mothering. But the angular formations in all zones—the loop of the *g* in *morning* in the first line; the *m* in *mist* in the first line;

the *t*-crossing in *Onto* in the second line; the *k* in *sky* in the third line; the *l* and the *d* in *field* in the fourth line . . . and many other sharp, piercing angular formations—show overwhelming anger and aggression. In a relationship, this guy would undoubtedly demand unconditional mothering—and when this impossible need was not met, his rage would surface and destroy any feelings of love.

Dr. Robert Sternberg has said that "a strong emotional commitment is essential to a long-term relationship." So . . . before you put your furniture in storage and move in with your lover . . . before you buy an engagement ring or set a wedding date . . . analyze your prospective partner's handwriting to determine the *quality* of his or her commitment. If the writing shows the ability to make a mature commitment, consider yourself fortunate—you will have a responsible and responsive mate. If they are only capable of sentimental commitment, expect your relationship to change as they develop new values and experience personal growth. If they can only make a dependent commitment, the prognosis will be poor if you don't like to be leaned on. And if your heart's desire is truly incapable of commitment, ponder the possibility that you might be subjecting yourself to suffering . . . and consider another candidate for your love.

8 Parental Influences

My heart belongs to Daddy. Mama's boy. Portnoy complex.

You don't have to be a champion of Freudian psychiatry to allow that a child's relationship with Mom and Dad influences his attitudes toward girl and boy, woman and man.

Contemporary psychologists are avidly investigating the ways in which a person's childhood shapes the romantic nature.

In a 1985 New York Times *article called "Patterns of Love Charted in Studies," psychology writer Daniel Goleman summarized some preliminary findings.*

Dr. Mary Ainsworth of the University of Virginia reported that "infants who feel that their mother is available and responsive are secure as lovers. Those who feel insecure about being loved fall into two patterns, either anxious and clinging or withdrawing."

Dr. Philip Shaver of the University of Denver concurred that secure lovers were "secure children." In their adult love relationships, they are "happy and trusting." Children of "emotionally intrusive mothers and distant fathers" become "anxious lovers," prone to obsession, jealousy and emotional extremes—or else tending to avoid intimacy.

Dr. Carl Hindy of the University of North Florida in Jacksonville found that people with problems in adult love relationships frequently had rejecting, hostile or inconsistent parents. Men who become "overinvested in their lovers, and who complained their affection is not sufficiently returned by their partner had mothers who were relatively uninvolved with them as children."

Women who were "similarly overinvested" had "detached, even hostile fathers."

Makes sense, doesn't it, that in our adult life we "act out" that familiar experience of pleasure or pain?

Take the case of the woman who was always "Daddy's Little Princess."
While her girlfriends complained about meeting "creeps," she gravitated
toward men who adored her.

Consider the attentive husband whose wife periodically accuses him of
"emotional neglect." Sometimes he wonders if she's "really" addressing her
father, a compulsive gambler given to frequent disappearances.

And how about the teenager whose boyfriend constantly complains that
she doesn't say "I love you" enough. Could he expect her verbal assurances to
compensate for his lonely, foster-home childhood?

In handwriting analysis, you can see how the writer's relationships with
both mother and father have influenced the psychological development.
Naturally, this knowledge can't predict a person's behavior in romantic
relationships. Even the "love pattern" experts agree that "people are not
doomed by their childhoods . . ." and that "a couple's ability to communicate
with each other . . . can be as important for the success of a relationship as
their childhood experiences."

In any attempt at psychological analysis, one must take into account the
individual's adaptation to experience. A child of divorced parents could
become cynical about marriage and reject intimate relationships . . . or this
same person could make a harmonious, stable marriage a major priority. The
son of an angry, domineering mother could be afraid of women . . . or he
could pursue gentle, even-tempered supportive partners to dote on. The
daughter of an abusive father may uncannily attract exploiters . . . or she
could let a sensitive, loving man teach her how to trust.

When we look at the Lovestrokes that reveal the writer's parental
influences, we use our insights to predict probable behavior patterns based on
the other information we have about the writer's psychology.

Parental influences are seen in the movements and trends in the
handwriting.

MOVEMENTS AND TRENDS

Symbolically speaking, the left represents the mother, and her influence,
and the right, the father.

This assumption is derived from the fact that, with each sentence
you write, you *begin* at the *left* side of a page and *move* to the *right*.

Each of us begins life with the mother. Whether or not you were
adopted at birth, conceived by a surrogate parent or had a mother who

abandoned you in infancy or died during childbirth, the mother still represents one's origins.

In the next phase of development—the future—the infant forms a relationship with the father, and then, subsequently, with other family members and the outside world.

Graphology interprets each handwritten page as a picture of the writer's unconscious. When you move your pen from left to right, you reveal your feelings about your origins (mother) and your future (father).

When we analyze the influence of the parents, we look at trends, or movements to the right or left in the upper and lower zones.

Left movements, or left trends, symbolize the writer's relations to the mother . . . and the past.

Right movements, or right trends, tell about the role of the father . . . and the writer's feelings about the future and the world at large.

"Normal," "healthy" psychological adjustment indicates that the writer moves purposefully into the future, as a handwriting should ideally move energetically toward the right margin.

Good rightward movement shows a good adjustment to the father to the outside world, and to the future. Here is an example of good rightward movement.

But when its all said and done, its really not such a bad place afterall.

Good Rightward Movement

Conversely, this next sample shows resistance of rightward movement.

Sometimes I wonder just why the world persists in doing what it does. The sun rises

Resistance of Rightward Movement

A resistance of rightward movement could show difficulties with the father, or a possible excessive involvement with the mother.

Trends are apparent in the lower and upper zones. In the upper zone, they are seen in *t*-crossings and *i*-dots. In the lower zone, they are seen in the loops.

The *t*-crossings in the following sample show right trend in the upper zone.

RIGHT TREND

day-time sometimes in the nighttime, but

LEFT TREND

The lower loop of the *y* in *day,* which does not move right to close at the base line, is an example of the left trend in the lower zone.

The zone in which a trend—or a lack of a trend—appears shows the area of conflict or adjustment.

Right trends are appropriate to the movement of the handwriting. Therefore, right trends in any zone show involvement with the father and his influence. Left trends in any zone show involvement with the mother, and possible avoidance of the father.

TRENDS IN THE LOWER ZONE

Good right trends in the lower zone show a healthy psychological adjustment to both parents.

represent my on-going education -- and they are very important to me.

Good Right Trends in Lower Zone

See how these close and continue with a stroke to the right. Left trends in the lower zone show unresolved conflicts with the mother.

Drifting left lower loops show a need for mothering. Instead of descending vertically, as would be appropriate to the movement of the handwriting, the loop strays over to the left margin—to the mother. In male handwritings, this may indicate a need for unconditional "mother love" from his mate.

equally you swing away years

Left-Drifting Lower Zone Loops (from four different male writers)

Angular loops show unresolved anger toward the mother. In male handwritings, this could indicate a tendency toward aggression toward women in their romantic and sexual relationships.

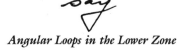

Angular Loops in the Lower Zone

Left-drifting, unclosed loops show that the writer's mother never lived up to the child's expectations and are an indication of resulting immaturity.

Left-Drifting, Unclosed Loops

TRENDS IN THE UPPER ZONE

Right trends in the upper zone, seen in rightward-extending *t*-crossings, show a good adaptation to the father's value system.

Good Upper Zone Right Trend

Left trends in the upper zone, seen in leftward-extending *t*-crossings, and *i*'s dotted to the left, show that the writer has conflicts with the father's value system or prefers the values of the mother.

Left-Trend T-Crossing

Left-Trend I-Dot

PARENTAL INFLUENCES

Let's analyze some sample handwritings to see the effect of the parental influences by integrating our observations of movements and trends with all the other graphological indicators of Lovestrokes Analysis.

The handwriting of this journalist clearly shows problematic relationships with both parents. The vertical writing and lack of rightward movement, left trend in the upper zone seen in leftward *t*-crossings, show an aversion to the father and a clash with his value system. Unresolved anger and tension with the maternal relationship are also seen in the angular lower zone loops. This combination of unresolved anger toward both parents contributes to the feeling of tension and rigidity in the handwriting, seen through angular formations, excessive vertical movement, twisting letter formations and lower loops that close below the base line.

With such a high level of hostility and frustration, romantic patterns will invariably be affected. The extremely wide margin tells you that he avoids intimacy—perhaps because he's afraid of his own anger.

Male, Age Thirty-seven

The handwriting of this political analyst contains good movements and trends in both upper and lower zones, showing a healthy adjustment to the values and influences of both parents. The writing shows creative, simplified forms and even spacing, revealing superior intelligence and good judgment. Lower loops that close at the base line show comfort with unconscious impulses and sexual drives. Because the writing is so rounded, we can conclude that he is empathic, emotional and expressive. In conclusion, this writer has positively assimilated the influences of both parents. Undoubtedly, he would be a sweet, supportive, affectionate and passionate mate.

When I lived in New York I swore I'd live nowhere else. And then I saw it — life elsewhere. It exists! But how? Differently. But that's because its elsewhere.

It could be that it wasn't that far away to begin with. You don't know that until you leave. And then, its Too late!

Male, Age Thirty-two

The handwriting of this modern dancer is characterized by good right movement, high energy, roundedness, lower loops closing at the base line, and right trends in the upper zone. In the upper zone, right trends are seen in the extending *t*-crossings in the word *ancient* in the first line and *depict* in the second line. Right slant and right movement show extroversion and a need to make contact with others. Roundedness shows emotions and empathy. Lower loops closing at the base line show a lack of unconscious conflicts and healthy sexual desires. Taking everything into consideration, we can conclude that this friendly, warm, outgoing writer needs relationships, and that, since she has made a successful adjustment to her father, she is also capable of being a loving wife.

you'll get to see why the ancient clay sculptures of pregnant women depict women with huge thighs, hips and bellys and tiny arms, legs and head! I've never been so aware of the middle of my body as I am now. Even though "the dance" focuses on the Torso, this is real concentrated attention!

Female, Age Thirty-eight

The handwriting of this actress is characterized by middle zone emphasis, extreme lower zone loops, wide, even spaces between words, a lack of right trends, and right lower zone pressure. The extreme lower loops show emotional neediness; the lack of right trends shows a problematic relationship with the father. While she appears to be self-contained, even introverted (extremely wide spaces between words), the large, wide letters and large loops indicate that she wants to express her intense emotions. In a relationship with a man, she may initially have problems embracing intimacy (extreme spaces between words), but it's possible that when she develops trust in him, she will want him to "compensate" for what she didn't get from her father.

an ever-recurring omnipresent weed in the garden of my mind. It's not one of the flowers I cultivated, like the truly blue

Female, Age Thirty-one

These Lovestrokes Analyses of parental influences can only give clues to *possible* behavior patterns. Graphology can never predict how two people will interact . . . but it can provide a new explanation for past patterns and current conflicts.

9 IQ: Integrity Quotient

Some enchanted evening you may meet a stranger across a crowded room, on the commuter train or at the baseball game. He may introduce himself with a witty come-on line. She may flash you her most flirtatious smile. You're interested.

But how can you determine this stranger's intentions if you have no acquaintances in common?

Maybe he's just interested in casual sex.

Maybe she's just interested in finding a guy who will buy her dinner.

How high is this potential lover's IQ—integrity quotient?

HONEST CHARACTER

If your nature is honest and trusting, then you probably automatically expect other people to be on your level.

Romantic involvements with low IQ types can leave you bitter.

High IQ people who consistently attract low IQ'ers may eventually give up on love altogether. They convince themselves that career success or creative pursuits are far more gratifying than any relationship.

This is ironic, because people with the highest IQs shine their brightest through loving and being loved. High IQ people identify with others. This ability to empathize enables them to be caring, sensitive partners, who wish to avoid inflicting emotional pain and who strive to keep communications clear and clean. High IQ types "do unto others as they would have others do unto them." When they violate their own strong principles, they usually feel guilty and remorseful and initiate efforts to make amends. High IQ lovers include partners who like to talk things out. When they sense that a third party is needed to clear up emotional confusion, they willingly enter psychotherapy, sex therapy or marriage counseling.

The high IQ handwriting will have an open, honest "look." It is characterized by clear, well-defined forms without signs of neglect, well-balanced zones, legibility, and a possible upper zone emphasis.

Well, what can you do? Remembering's one thing — associating's another.

High Integrity

This handwriting has extreme legibility and clearness. The three zones are balanced, and the spatial arrangement is excellent. Thus, we can conclude that the writer has an honest, open character, and prefers truthfulness to subterfuge.

I decided to throw a party in celebration of my promotion. Guess what, none of the men showed up. But, in New York that's not hard to believe Now I'm in the

High Integrity

While this handwriting is also clear and legible, with good balance between the three zones, it is also quite controlled. Arcade formations and narrow lower loops show restraint and inhibition. There are good extensions into the upper zone, showing idealism, yet schooltype forms show conventionality. This writer adheres to the strict moral standards she was raised with. The integrity quotient is high, but the happiness quotient may be low.

SMOOTH OPERATORS

If you have a Mensa-qualifying IQ, then you might be an easy mark for a *smooth operator,* whose behavior may be manipulative.

To some extent, everyone is manipulative. Infants learn to manipulate their parents by throwing tantrums, crying and sulking—or by giving hugs and kisses. As adults, we find ourselves in situations that require manipulation: convincing your parents to lend you money, your teacher to give you a higher grade, your boss to grant you extra vacation days, your landlord permission to keep a pet in your apartment.

In romantic relationships, there will often be situations that require manipulation—like giving your lover a compliment before making a demand, or giving a gift before breaking bad news.

But for some people, manipulation is their normal modus operandi.

The classic smooth operator has low self-esteem and believes that good things come from without rather than within. He is always looking to get things from others, and when he gives, he gives with strings attached. A smooth operator requires a weak partner who can be made to feel guilty. Temper tantrums, acting hurt and sulking are effective instruments. A smooth operator may suffer from pangs of conscience, but eventually he will revert to "looking out for number one."

What motivates the smooth operator?

Some were oversensitive children who got their feelings hurt so often that they developed their ability to manipulate as coping mechanism. Many were themselves manipulated by parents or siblings and grew up with deceit as a standard of normal behavior. Other smooth operators are simply emotionally cool. They prefer games to honesty. The demands of an intimate relationship only irritate them.

During courtship and dating, a smooth operator will pressure his partner into having sex before she feels "ready"; she will "con" him into spending money on her. In the context of a long-term relationship, the smooth operator usually ends up getting his way, be the issue household chores, financial contributions, relations with relatives and in-laws, child-care responsibilities.

For example, it wasn't until his divorce had been finalized that Andy consciously realized that Terry had always decided when they would have sex. Whenever he initiated lovemaking, she discouraged him with an irrefutable argument, like: "Why don't we wait until Friday night, honey? You know that I always feel more relaxed at the end of the workweek . . . and that makes our sex so much more erotic!"

When Grace met Jimmy, he was unemployed and chronically depressed. He convinced her that he "needed" her to take care of him. Grace was flattered, and the Girl Scout in her wanted to "help" Jimmy, to teach him to become self-sufficient. After three years of lending money and cleaning his apartment, Grace concluded that Jimmy would "never get his act together."

Tears, tantrums, denial of sex have always been traditional techniques of female manipulation. Confessions of neediness, flattery and seduction have been male methods. But both men and women are capable of using the tool of manipulation that best serves their purposes.

The graphological indicators of the smooth operator are: confusion between the three zones, a small or neglected middle zone and a combination of thread and angle connections.

- *Confusion between the three zones* shows changing values and quickly changing needs.
- *A small or neglected middle zone,* in conjunction with these other factors, shows low self-esteem.
- *Thread connections* show the intuitive ability to understand other people—and therefore to know how to make them feel guilty.
- *Angles* show aggression and the desire to get one's needs met.

Here are examples of two handwritings that show all the graphological indicators of the smooth operator:

Smooth Operators

Interestingly, in the second sample, we see a downhill slant, indicating depression, which might possibly be a consequence of low self-esteem.

GIVE YOURSELF AN "IQ QUIZ"

Look at your own handwriting.

- Is it clear and legible?
- Does it show regularity and good spacing?
- Are the zones balanced, with possible emphasis on the upper zone?
- Then your IQ puts you in the top 10 percent of the population!
- Does it show irregularities in form?
- Is there a combination of threads and angles?
- Are the zones confused? Is the middle zone small?

Then you may manipulate infrequently, or constantly. Even if you aspire to honest communication, inner compulsions pull you toward deceit. Trying to improve your self-esteem is critical to becoming a better mate.

10 Hidden Troubles, Hidden Charms: Things Your Lover Never Told You

A *Lovestrokes Analysis* can provide you with all sorts of insights into the psychosexual dynamics and social functioning of a partner or prospective partner. Taken one step further, *Lovestrokes* can pinpoint personality traits that are so serious—and so subtle—that your discoveries may be absolutely astonishing.

Violent tendencies, addictive personality makeup, compulsive behavior may never manifest outwardly. Or you may one day find out that your boyfriend or girlfriend, husband or wife, has hidden troubles too shameful to admit.

Hidden charms can also be exposed through a *Lovestrokes Analysis*. Often a controlled façade can conceal a warm heart and a generous spirit. Should you pursue a person whose attitude is standoffish, whose demeanor is aloof?

The *Things Your Lover Never Told You* include both hidden troubles and hidden charms. If you're curious about your romantic compatibility, you should be prepared to face the shocking truths . . . or the encouraging news.

HIDDEN TROUBLES

VIOLENT TENDENCIES

Tom was a regular churchgoer and active in the PTA. One day, he sent his wife of three years to the hospital with a cracked rib and a broken collarbone.

Many violent people are excellent actors, capable of masking their feelings of aggression for long periods of time. Some never reveal their

LOVE "LETTERS"

$\mathcal{E}$	Cultural interests	The "Greek" *e*
∂	Writing ability	The lyrical *d*
m	Visual sense	Strong, archlike arcades
f	In a woman, maternal instincts	Small *f* with a big lower loop
$\mathcal{Y}$	High intellect	Figure-eight *g*
$\mathcal{J}$	Musical ability	Music-note *d*
$\mathcal{Y}$	Consciousness about weight or sensitivity to touch	Big lower loop crossing through the base line
$\mathcal{I}$	Creative talent	Block capital *I*
$\vert$	Independent thinker	Ultrasimplified capital *I*
$\mathcal{G}$	Strong mother influence	Big upper loop capital *I*
$i\mathcal{t}$	Superior intellect	Lower-case *i* dotted by *t*-crossing
$\overset{\circ}{\imath}$	Immaturity, a need for attention	Circular *i* dot

"demons," others get out their anger by hitting a wall or a punching bag. Sometimes, though, a violent person under stress, or undergoing an emotional trauma, will "snap," and direct that rage toward a vulnerable target.

The graphological indicators for violent tendencies are: lots of angles, excessive pressure, sudden stoppages, changes of direction, increased pressure at the end of a stroke and "clubstrokes."

The *angles* and *heavy pressure* show inner aggression; *sudden stoppages* in the flow of the writing show emotional volatility; *changes of direction* show loss of emotional control; and *increased pressure at the end of a stroke or clubstrokes* show pressure—or anger—directed toward others.

Here is an example of angularity and heavy pressure.

Wait it out.

Here is an example of a sudden stoppage. The small *t* in the word *but* should return to the base line and curve out to the right.

but I don't

Here are two examples of changes in direction.

don't   I am not here to

Here is an example of an endstroke with increased pressure.

Onto the

And this is an example of a clubstroke. It is a thick, solid bar.

it will.

The signatures of famous criminals show these graphological indicators.

Nazi leader Heinrich Himmler, who was head of the SS and the Gestapo, shows ultra extreme angularity and clubstroke crossings in his signature.

Mark David Chapman signed John Lennon's signature on a document shortly before shooting him. Note the heavy pressure and endstrokes with increased pressure. In this particular example, the endstroke returns in a self-destructive circle through the signature, symbolically "canceling it out."

ADDICTIVE PERSONALITIES

On their third anniversary, Joel decided to surprise Clara by baking a cake. Searching through the pantry shelf, he discovered a bottle of vodka wedged in between a can of sugar and a bag of flour.

Addictive personalities have difficulties in controlling their impulses. If drugs and alcohol offer them pleasure and opportunity to escape from unpleasant realities, or an excuse for avoiding responsibilities, then they will have trouble resisting them. But graphological indicators showing a potentially addictive personality do not decree a verdict of guilty. Addictive personalities can sublimate unhealthy addictions into healthy addictions—like the woman "cured" of an eating disorder who becomes a "fitness freak."

The graphological indicators for the addictive personality are: a lack of control, irregularity, variability in zones, zone interference, t-crossings in the middle zone.

- The *lack of control* in the handwriting shows lack of self-control in general.
- *Irregularity* shows the willingness to avoid discipline and to give in to impulses.
- *Variability in zones* and *zone interference* show value confusion, and thus the capacity to make "the wrong choice."

- Lower-case t-*crossings that extend through the middle zone* show self-destructive tendencies.

Let's look at an example of a potentially addictive personality.

The handwriting of this male musician shows all the addictive personality indicators, combined with a widening left margin (lavishness). His "addiction" is chain-smoking cigarettes.

COMPULSIVE BEHAVIOR

During their year-long engagement, Carl had noticed that his fiancée's apartment was always tidy. Still, he was shocked when his new bride ironed their bedsheets and scrubbed the kitchen floor on her hands and knees before retiring.

The compulsive personality may be compulsive about exercising, career achievements or overeating. Such behavior is relatively harmless, and most of us have some compulsive tendencies. In more extreme cases, compulsive behaviors dominate the person's life, and can lead to anorexia, gambling, kleptomania, workaholism.

The graphological indicators of compulsive behavior are seen when a handwriting is rigidly repetitious.

Rigid repetition means that the exact same letter formations are made repeatedly.

Here is an example of a compulsive personality whose handwriting is rigidly repetitious.

The tight, rigid, closed, controlled, repetitious forms in the handwriting of this female homemaker show that any deviation from her orderly routines will provoke great anxiety.

HIDDEN CHARMS

Naturally, not all hidden Lovestrokes have negative connotations. Hidden Lovestrokes can also strip away a deceptive façade. When Gary met Cynthia, he found her remote and aloof, but intriguing. So he pursued her . . . and eventually learned that she was warm, loyal and loving.

When Sonia met Ted, he seemed so self-contained that she assumed he was self-centered. He pursued her . . . and she ended up with a devoted, supportive husband.

SHY BUT LOVING

People who are shy but loving may be either self-conscious with others, or extremely discriminating and selective. When someone proves worthy of their trust, they will respond with emotional enthusiasm.

The graphological indicators for the shy but loving personality would be extremely wide spaces between words combined with roundedness.

Here is an example of a shy but loving handwriting.

Pichet-line Priscilla crawled in printwriting. Suddenly, three shots rang out . . . .

The vertical writing shows poise and self-containment, and the extremely wide spaces between words show a difficulty making emotional connections to others in the handwriting of this male disc jockey. But rounded forms and large, rounded lower loops show emotional neediness and a sweet, loving nature.

CAUTIOUS BUT GENEROUS

Some people seem to be so cautious and methodical that one assumes they would make a better research scientist than a mate. But if the handwriting shows good character, this person simply needs time to decide about whether to make a commitment. Once committed, he will carefully try to understand his mate, and to generously meet her needs.

Here is an example of a cautious but generous handwriting.

dangerous or pointless? For the same reason I once showed my hand to a palmist: out of intellectual curiosity. Surprising, the things

The forms in the handwriting of this male editor are extremely precise and restrained. Vertical writing shows self-containment. But even spacing between words, good legibility and clarity in the middle zone, and balance between the three zones all indicate high integrity, and thus the ability to make a mature commitment. The widening left margin shows a generous nature, and wide, even spaces between lines confirm his idealism and the desire to be an admirable mate.

Hidden Lovestrokes must be evaluated carefully.

An occasional change of slant could mean moodiness, not meanness.

Middle zone *t*-crossings could show temporary self-destructive feelings based on guilt, stress or trauma.

Heavy pressure could mean supersensuousness.

So, before you ship your spouse off to the Betty Ford Rehab Center, or tip off the FBI about a potential assassin, look at all the other Lovestrokes in the handwriting for insight into values, integrity and emotional makeup to arrive at a balanced evaluation.

11 "Personals" Penmanship: Finding Love Through the Classifieds

Years ago, people assumed that anyone placing or answering a "Personals" ad was a loser or a weirdo. Today, most newspapers and many magazines across the country contain "Personals" sections. Finding love, or just an interesting date, through letter-writing is as socially acceptable as attending a college mixer.

If you're considering placing a "Personals" ad, your knowledge of Lovestrokes will transform the entire process. Request only handwritten responses on unlined paper. Your Lovestrokes Analysis will enable you to zero in on the truly eligible and to eliminate all inappropriate candidates.

Naturally, most respondents will employ the art of self-promotion. They will describe themselves as intelligent, sensitive and irresistible—when they might actually be self-centered and overbearing.

Ruth Brayer, a certified graphologist and the president of Graphological Services International, with offices in New York City and Woodmere, Long Island, uses graphology in her practice as a management consultant and in her specialized service for placers of "Personals" ads.

Among her clients are single women between the ages of twenty-five and fifty who advertise in magazines. Her male clients generally come for counseling about ongoing relationships—although a few fellows have asked her to screen their "Personals" responses.

First, Brayer analyzes the client's handwriting, to get a sense of "what makes them tick" and also to determine their needs and priorities. Then she screens their responses (which average around forty) and selects seven writers who show the highest potential for romantic compatibility.

Here are some of her true-life tales:

A middle-aged divorcée got twenty replies to her magazine ad. Brayer analyzed her writing and deduced from her right slant and narrow, even spaces between words that she had strong needs for intimacy and communication in her relationships.

Fortunately, one of the respondents' handwriting also had a right slant, combined with rounded forms, garland connections, and lots of loops. The two have been a "steady item" for months.

A woman in her early twenties received ten responses to her newspaper ad, but was intrigued by the content of one in particular. Brayer noted extremely large capitals, a neglected middle zone and writing that went so far out to the right margin that "it practically ran off the page."

"This is a man of extremes," Brayer cautioned. "He's looking for thrills."

Nonetheless, the client dated him. A month later, she telephoned to report that her new friend had left town—to pursue a trek up Mt. Everest!

Another woman Brayer describes as "indecisive" received a flood of replies and called men in alphabetical order before seeking "Personals" counseling. She showed Brayer the letter of a man with whom she had had a lengthy political argument over the phone.

"You're crazy to give up on this one!" Brayer exclaimed. "This guy is the best you've got—intelligent, receptive and warm."

His handwriting showed clarity and legibility, rounded, even loops in the upper and lower zones, and excellent spacing.

Eventually, the client decided that integrity was more important to her than ideology, and contacted the man to suggest a rendezvous. Now, on Election Days, husband and wife vote for different candidates, but they endorse each other's right to an opposing opinion.

Usually, "success stories" report to Brayer only sporadically.

"It's like going to a doctor," Brayer says. "When things are going well, and you're feeling healthy, you don't call him."

"Disaster Dates," however, often inspire immediate feedback.

A woman in her late thirties who had described herself as "vivacious and voluptuous" received sixty-five replies to her magazine ad. Brayer singled out seven hot prospects. But the client insisted that her first choice would be a successful businessman whose enclosed photo revealed movie-star good looks.

"Keep away from him," Brayer warned. "Sure, he's intelligent and successful, but underneath he's a mama's boy, very passive and emotionally immature."

She drew her conclusions by observing his disorganized, narrow writing, with drifting left lower zone loops and returning left endstrokes, combined with an overemphasized upper zone.

Nonetheless, the client went out to dinner with him, and when he brought her home, she invited him up for a drink.

She called Brayer the next day.

"He was like a piece of wood in bed," she groused. "He wanted me to do all the work."

Generalizing from her experience, Brayer says that many men who reply to "Personals" are "the nervous type."

Their margins, spacing, forms and size of letters are all irregular.

"Women are attracted by men whose handwritings are highly irregular because, at the beginning, they are fun and exciting," says Brayer. "But those very qualities speak against long-term love affairs. Their unpredictability is an aspect of their lack of perseverance."

Instead, she offers these recommendations to "Personals" ads placers of both sexes. She calls them Ruth's Rules.

RUTH'S RULES

- Don't read the lines . . . read between the lines.
- If you see overlappings between the three zones and lots of extremes, watch out!
- Don't be fooled by a large signature—it might mean a small ego.
- Your best bet will be a handwriting that is regular but not rigid, spontaneous but not erratic, and has good movement and balance between the three zones.

And if you're considering answering a "Personals" ad, why not try something original, like a humorous postcard? A hardworking single man or woman who comes home exhausted after a busy day at the office might not have the patience to give each letter in a stack a careful reading. Keep your signature modest in size, and don't try to embellish or alter your natural handwriting in order to make a "good impression." After all, your mystery Ms. or Mr. Write might have read this book . . . and will be looking at your Lovestrokes!

12 Celebrity Signatures: A Look at Thirteen Famous Lovestrokes

A signature alone is not sufficient for an in-depth graphological analysis. In the interest of accuracy, the signature must be evaluated in the context of a two-paragraph handwriting sample.

In the case of celebrities, however, a signature takes on enhanced significance. Athletes, actors, musicians and politicians perfect a John Hancock that they hope will express their uniqueness and satisfy autograph seekers.

Have you ever wondered whether the established "sex symbols" you admire are as hot as their hype? Have you ever speculated about the sexual "life-styles of the rich and famous" when they're off-screen, off-stage, off the playing field and off the podium? Does Madonna appear before her audiences attired in lingerie for shock value, or because she loves lacy bras? A casual restaurant lunch with Barbara Walters catalyzed former secretary of state Henry Kissinger's reputation as a ladies' man—but is he?

Let's look at the Lovestrokes in thirteen celebrity signatures. The categories will be Actors and Actresses, Rock Stars, Athletes and Politicians.

ACTORS AND ACTRESSES

1. MARILYN MONROE

A talented actress and comedienne whose inner torment eventually drove her to suicide, Marilyn Monroe will probably always be considered the ultimate sex goddess—the archetype of a voluptuous, gorgeous woman who radiates sexuality.

Married to playwright Arthur Miller and Hall of Fame Yankees outfielder Joe DiMaggio, she was also rumored to have had illicit romantic relationships with two of the Kennedy brothers, John and Robert.

To determine whether the "real" Monroe was a true sex goddess, or sexually neurotic, let's look at the Lovestrokes in her signature.

An abiding interest in sex is certainly indicated in her signature (she only signed her first name). The lower loop of the y is extremely pronounced, and the formations of the capital M are quite rounded. She brings the middle zone strokes of the M way down into the lower zone of sex and the unconscious. These formations create a flamboyant, original signature.

The middle zone letters, in comparison to the capital M, are actually quite narrow, a sign of shyness and inhibition. Because her writing has a right slant, it can be assumed that she was always attempting to overcome her basic introversion. The endstroke of the n is inappropriately long and heavy, indicating that she made a conscious effort to reach out to people despite her natural introverted inclinations.

Now let's take a closer look at that unusual lower loop. Notice how she makes a tiny angle and then the loop. The loop goes straight out to the left and remains way below the base line. The angle shows ambivalent feelings about sex and possible past sexual trauma. The malformed, exaggerated loop shows that, while sexuality was a constant preoccupation with her, she remained sexually unfulfilled, frustrated and confused.

2. ELIZABETH TAYLOR

Widely considered "the most beautiful woman in the world," this adored actress is renowned for an extraordinary career that commenced during her childhood; her tempestuous and passionate love affairs and marriages have also continued to fascinate fans. She and Richard Burton were married twice and divorced twice, and their love affair was one of the most glamorous pairings in Hollywood history.

Let's take a look at the Lovestrokes in her signature.

A Lovestrokes expert might assume that the extreme illegibility of this signature has negative connotations. Actually, although the forms are illegible, they are highly stylized and creative, produced with great speed and facility.

Taylor's illegibility is symbolic of an attitude of superiority; she doesn't feel the necessity to reveal herself or to make her "real" self clear to others. She doesn't give a damn what other people think of her. The speed shows that she energetically pursues her own goals.

The returning left endstrokes of her first name show self-involvement and an acquisitive nature.

Is she sexy?

Absolutely.

The extreme roundedness of the writing shows a sensuous nature; long lower zone extensions show comfort with sexual impulses.

Why has she had so many husbands?

The irregularity of the writing, combined with the speed, shows that she can be easily bored and needs variety. She could even be categorized as a "short-term romantic."

3. KATHARINE HEPBURN

Multiple-Oscar-winner Katharine Hepburn is considered to be one of the greatest actresses in American history. Her versatility and consummate professionalism have been much lauded; off-camera and off-stage she projects the image of a strong-minded Yankee individualist. Although she never married, she sustained an enduring companionship with her favorite co-star, the great Spencer Tracy.

Let's look at the Lovestrokes in Hepburn's signature.

This extremely simplified, stylish, sophisticated and creative signature shows a great degree of unconventionality. Hepburn lives by her own rules, does things her own way and sets her own tempo. The upper zone emphasis and lack of loops or roundedness would suggest that intellectual pursuits and the effective use of her talents are a greater priority than sexual expression.

4. WHOOPI GOLDBERG

Once upon a time, a single parent was so broke that she took a job as a beautician in a morgue. Then director Mike Nichols "discovered" her and brought her one-woman comedy show to Broadway. Using the name "Whoopi Goldberg," she performed poignant but humorous characterizations of California teen-agers, "street people" and the handicapped. Next came a starring role—and an Oscar nomination—in the film *The Color Purple,* and a Grammy Award for the Best Comedy Album of 1985. Soon, Whoopi Goldberg was considered the most desirable new actress in Hollywood. Her public persona has always been offbeat and irreverent; she accepted a Golden Globe Award wearing jogging pants. A supportive public is wondering exactly who is this elusive, oddly named lady. And how interested is she in "making Whoopi"?

Let's look at the Lovestrokes in her signature.

Despite her iconoclastic demeanor, Goldberg's signature shows a strong schooltype influence. Because her basic nature is conventional, she is probably attracted to true "nonconformists," hoping that their influence will rub off on her. The writing is extremely regular, showing strong discipline. Roundedness shows strong sensuality, but the extreme regularity also reveals high standards. Whoopi is very selective and choosy about picking partners.

5. BURT REYNOLDS

He created controversy by dating an "older woman"—Dinah Shore. His other ladyloves have included Sally Field and Loni Anderson.

A fine actor, Reynolds projects an image that combines strength and gentleness, sex appeal and sensitivity—the ultimate "high-consciousness" eighties man.

Who is the *real* Burt Reynolds? Let's look at the Lovestrokes in his signature.

The extreme right slant shows the potential for emotional dependency in love relationships. The writing is speedy and energetic, full of vitality. The middle zone formations of the capital letters descend deep into the lower zone. He appears to be a man of strong sexual drives who possesses the vitality to be an energetic lover. But the narrow lower loop of the y hints that he might also be a bit shy sexually, and the lower zone angle in the capital R, combined with such strong pressure, hints that he might encourage friction in sexual relationships.

6. DON JOHNSON

Consummately cool and hiply handsome, Don Johnson, the star of the innovative TV cop show "Miami Vice," became an instant sex symbol. One company developed a razor that would produce a Johnson-esque one-day beard stubble. Men across America emulated his fashion sensibility—expensive Italian suits worn with T-shirts and without socks.

How similar is Don Johnson, the man, to Sonny Crockett, the intensely attractive cop he portrays on television?

Let's look at the Lovestrokes in his signature.

Because the initial capital letters in his signature are extremely large, we can assume that Johnson is quite conscious of the way he appears to others. The huge loop of the J that encircles his first name reflects an acquisitive nature, the desire to keep things for himself. This encirclement also reveals self-confusion. The forms are rounded and made with heavy pressure, showing sensuality and vitality. But the irregularity of the forms shows a need for variety. At heart, he might be a "short-term romantic."

7. ROCK HUDSON

When he died a tragic death from AIDS, it was finally admitted that Rock Hudson, one of Hollywood's handsomest heartthrobs, a man of rugged, all-American good looks, had been a homosexual. He had convincingly played the leading man to many of the world's most beautiful women. As the "real" story of Hudson's life was revealed, the public learned of his bitterness over having to hide his homosexuality in the pre–gay liberation era.

Can a savvy graphologist detect homosexuality in Hudson's Hancock?

Let's look at the Lovestrokes in his signature.

Writing that is this carefully crafted, slow and precise, indicating the need to make a deliberate impression on others, is known as "persona" writing. It's difficult to see what is "between the lines." People develop "persona" signatures in order to hide their true natures. A "persona" signature in this case is yet another symbol of the fact that Hudson was forced to live a lie.

ROCK STARS

8. BRUCE SPRINGSTEEN

He's nicknamed "The Boss"—because his millions of fans consider singer/songwriter Bruce Springsteen—known for his intelligent, poetic and socially astute lyrics and energetic performances—to be the ultimate rock-and-roller. Although he wrote scores of love songs, Springsteen remained a bachelor into his late thirties before settling down with gorgeous model/actress Julianne Phillips.

Was he waiting to meet his soulmate—or did he enjoy the single life?

Let's look at the Lovestrokes in his signature.

*A small, somewhat illegible middle zone might indicate that, despite his innumerable successes, The Boss is still a bit insecure. Wide spaces between letters show the need for privacy, and thus a requirement for an independent mate. Most revealing of all is the double valentine formed in the capital **B**. The Boss is so romantic that we can assume his touching love lyrics are truly "heartfelt."*

9. MADONNA

She's been idolized and criticized, lauded for her creativity and dismissed as a sex object.

With a string of chart-topping hit records, Madonna, the woman who performed in lingerie and eroticized crucifixes by wearing them as earrings, has provoked intense emotional reactions. Married to fellow actor Sean Penn, Madonna remains an enigma. Is she an original talent, or a lucky trend-setter? Is she as sexy as her style of dress suggests?

Let's look at the Lovestrokes in her signature.

*The clever, unusual and original form of her capital **M** shows originality and creativity. Fast, energetic writing is the mark of a*

quick mind. The long, fearless descent of the middle zone formation
of the M into the lower zone reveals genuine interest in sex and
eroticism. But because the writing is so sophisticated, we can
conclude that Madonna is a woman who could enjoy being seduced
by a clever man.

ATHLETES

10. WILLIAM "THE REFRIGERATOR" PERRY

Genial, good-natured Chicago Bears defensive lineman William Perry is so popular that his income from commercial endorsements exceeds his salary. His scale-tipping girth has earned him the nickname "The Refrigerator" and inspired a whole new category of cheerleaders: the lively "Refrigerettes" are united in their obesity.

Fans may wonder . . . is The Refrigerator as interested in sex as he is in football and food?

Let's take a look at the Lovestrokes in his signature.

Vitality and threadiness characterize this signature. The
rhythm is smooth, indicating great efficiency. The large capital P
descends into the lower zone with a wide loop. While the lower loop
of the y is small and narrow, it is made forcefully, a sign of intense
sexual drives. Smoothness and fluidity show that The Refrigerator is
"pleasure-oriented" . . . and we can conclude that he enjoys all
pleasures.

11. DWIGHT GOODEN

Sports fans and sports experts speculate that the young Mets pitcher Dwight Gooden may become one of the greatest pitchers in baseball history. Whenever he appears on the field, the stadium erupts into applause and cheers; even the fans of the opposing team pay homage to the incredible "Doctor K."

In an effort to avoid overexposure of this young genius, the Mets have discouraged Gooden from granting too many interviews or signing up to promote products. As a result, the public is fascinated to know what Gooden is "really like." And, given his uncanny physical prowess, ladies might wonder, "How sexy is Dwight Gooden?"

Let's look at the Lovestrokes in his signature.

Extreme simplification denotes high intelligence. The writing is precise but fast, a sign that he is quite conscientious and perfectionistic. High upper zone extensions show big ambitions and strict standards. A lack of space between letters hints at emotional shyness. The oversized capital D shows left trend and an attachment to the past and the mother. While strong right movement and heavy pressure show vitality and sexual energy, other indicators show that he sets rigid rules for himself and is highly disciplined. If he had to choose between self-indulgence and self-discipline, the latter would win out.

POLITICIANS

12. FIDEL CASTRO

Cuban president Fidel Castro is considered ultracharismatic by his populace. Handsome and talkative, forever smoking a Havana, he is known to be a ladies' man—a charming "Latin lover." Americans are made uneasy by this confirmed Communist. In interviews, he pontificates and puzzles his listeners. Can Americans ever understand his incredible popularity?

Let's look at the Lovestrokes in his signature.

Overly elaborate capitals and a general lack of simplification are consistent with Castro's overtalkativeness. The writing shows extremely heavy pressure and force, as well as angular formations. He wants control and power and nothing can interfere with his determination. The endstroke that descends forcefully into the lower zone shows interest in sex; but the preponderance of angles in the upper and middle zones are sure signs of aggression. Here is a typical "macho" man who wants his pleasure—on his own terms. His lovemaking style is probably more rough then gentle.

13. HENRY KISSINGER

Many people thought it was ironic when Henry Kissinger, President Richard Nixon's secretary of state, developed a reputation as a sex symbol. While his intellectual brilliance was widely admired, his physical appearance was more statesmanlike than glamorous.

Was Kissinger's sex symbol image just a media myth?

Let's look at the Lovestrokes in his signature.

Total threadiness with no middle zone formations whatsoever is the hallmark of the classic diplomat. He reveals nothing about himself but the suggestion of his first initials. Total thread shows craftiness and hidden motives. As for sexuality, the minimal descent into the lower zone is a clue that "kissing" is Kissinger's lowest priority.

Celebrity sexual signatures can only be speculative. A Lovestrokes Analysis may indeed be accurate, but only the celebrity, and the celebrity's partners, will ever know the accuracy of these insights.

13 The Lovestrokes Compatibility Questionnaire

You have learned basic handwriting analysis and the Lovestrokes that determine intimacy capacity, sexuality, romantic nature, compromisability, value systems, commitment capacity, parental influences, integrity and hidden traits.

Now, you are ready to compare your handwriting with another's, to determine your romantic, sexual and even marital compatibility potential.

Compatibility potential involves evaluating your requirements in a mate—and your own relationship priorities.

---

1. How much importance do you place on your social life?

> *Great importance.*
> *Enjoy socializing but need privacy.*
> *Prefer solitude.*

If your social life is of great importance to you, your handwriting probably shows a right slant. You will have the highest compatibility potential with a fellow right slanter, and the lowest compatibility with a left slant writer.

If you enjoy socializing but also require quiet nights at home, you will have the highest compatibility with a vertical writer who creates wide, even spaces between words.

And if you prefer privacy to partying, then look for a left slant writer who creates extremely wide spaces between words. You will have the lowest compatibility with a right or extreme right slant writer, especially one who creates narrow even or uneven spaces between words.

2. How much importance do you attach to "keeping up with the Joneses"?

Extremely important.

Fairly important.

Couldn't care less.

Concept distasteful.

If being one of the gang is extremely important to you, then your handwriting will probably show a strong schooltype influence. If it is fairly important, you will show a moderate schooltype influence.

Marital compatibility will be highest with a writer who shows either of these two tendencies.

However, if you answered, "Couldn't care less" or "Concept distasteful," then your handwriting is probably creative and original.

You would have a compatibility clash with any writer who shows either a strong or moderate schooltype influence.

Seek out a fellow creative writer.

3. How materialistic are you?

Love to consume.

Luxury lover.

Don't care a hoot about loot.

If you're an ardent consumer and proud of it, you will have the highest compatibility with a mate who also enjoys putting down the plastic. Look for a strong middle zone emphasis.

Luxury lover? Look for a mate who makes garland connections—this fellow sybarite will share your champagne tastes.

If you're not at all materialistic, you will be most compatible with a writer whose letter formations are extremely creative, has a lack of middle zone emphasis, and a possible upper zone emphasis. You will be least compatible with a schooltype writer with a strongly emphasized middle zone, extreme lower loops and a lack of upper zone formations.

4. How ambitious are you?

Extremely ambitious.

Fairly ambitious, but not major priority.

Content to just slide by, doing my thing.

If you're extremely ambitious, you might want to match wits with an achieving mate. You will have the highest compatibility with a writer who creates clear letter formations, a legible middle zone, high upper zone extensions and shows good spacing and organization.

If you're fairly ambitious, you might look for legible writing and a developed middle zone, combined with creative letter formations.

If you're content to just slide by, avoid schooltype writers with high upper zone extensions. Look for a fellow creative writer, who makes rounded forms and has a right slant—this person will offer you support instead of criticism.

5. How strong are your needs to communicate your feelings?

I need constant emotional interchange.

I like an occasional heart-to-heart.

I'd rather not be bothered.

If you need to communicate to preserve your sanity, then you will have your highest compatibility with a mate who has a right slant or extreme right slant, good spacing between words, wide letters and roundedness.

If communication is in the middle of your list of priorities, seek out a vertical writer who leaves wide, even spaces between words, and creates rounded forms.

If discussing your feelings turns you off, then you will have your highest compatibility with a left slant or vertical writer who makes extremely wide spaces between words and lines, creates an extremely wide right margin, and whose connective form is either angular or arcade.

6. Can you compromise?

> *Yes, easily.*
> *Yes, with difficulty.*
> *Not unless I'm forced to!*

If you're extremely flexible, you'll appreciate the emotional largess of another flexible writer, a person whose writing shows roundedness, garland or thread connective forms, a possible right slant and lots of loops.

If you're only somewhat flexible, seek out a thread writer, who will help you learn how to see both sides of the issue.

If you're a little Napoleon, you will only clash with a fellow angle writer. You'll intimidate a garland writer. But you may meet your match with an arcade writer who employs a vertical and rigidly regular writing.

7. Do you enjoy acting out sexual fantasies?

> *And how!*
> *Sometimes, for a change of pace.*
> *What a disgusting suggestion!*

If you're erotically experimental, then you'll be able to let your imagination wander with a writer whose forms are creative or irregular; whose writing descends to the bottom of the page; who creates wide letters with big lower loops, long lower zone extensions or varying lower zone formations.

If you're only occasionally inclined to experiment, then look for roundedness and good upper and lower zone extensions.

And if you're a sexual straight arrow, you'll have the highest sexual compatibility potential with a schooltype writer whose letter formations, including lower zone loops, are narrow.

8. How strong is your sex drive?

Torrid.

I'm content with one or two times a week.

I'd rather do needlepoint.

If you have a lusty libido, then you will have the highest compatibility potential with a writer who uses strong pressure, has good movement and creates deep lower zone formations.

If your sex drive is about average, then look for good pressure and moderate lower zone emphasis.

If you think sex is overrated, then search for a partner whose writing shows weak pressure, minimal movement and a middle or upper zone emphasis with a neglected middle zone.

9. Women—do you like a domineering sex partner?

Sweep me off my feet, Rhett.

I like equality in all areas—including the bedroom.

Totally conflicts with my feminist principles.

If you like a man to be sexually aggressive, then watch for a handwriting that shows strong pressure, lots of angles and possible angle formations in the lower zone. But beware—the presence of clubstrokes, sudden stoppages or abrupt changes in slant might mean that Mr. Good-in-Bed is also Mr. Goodbar!

If you want to be as sexually active as your partner, then you'll have the highest sexual compatibility with a man whose writing shows strong pressure and pronounced lower zone formations, but also roundedness (ability to empathize with your needs).

If you're a sexual feminist who requires that a man be as supportive of your sexual needs as he is of your career ambitions, then find a guy who employs an extreme right slant. If he makes left-drifting lower zone loops, he'll also let you take the lead.

10. Men—what constitutes your perfect "10"?

A woman who is as sexually aggressive as myself.

A woman who is an equal partner.

An old-fashioned girl who lets me lead the way.

If you like a lover who will respond intensely and also take charge sexually, then look for the writing of a lady who makes full lower loops, has vertical writing, creative forms and uses good pressure.

If mutual give-and-take is your thing, look for a lady whose writing has good pressure, right slant and narrow spaces between words with a well-developed lower zone.

If you want to be the boss, then your lady love will employ delicate pressure, create narrow letter formations and will probably be a school-type writer.

11. How "grounded" are you?

Solid as a rock.

Dependable, but open to change.

A dreamer.

If you value stability and reliability in a mate, then you will achieve your highest compatibility with a writer who has a clear, legible middle zone; creates excellent spatial arrangements and even margins.

If you're both reliable and flexible, and want a mate to be equally mellow, then look for the indicators that are mentioned above, combined with a lack of restraint and upper zone extensions (imagination) or creative forms.

And if you're a dreamer, stay away from a writer with an excessive middle zone emphasis. Look for a fellow creative writer whose upper zone is all important.

12. How independent are you?

A law unto myself.

A person who needs people.

A clinging vine.

If you're independent, you'll probably be turned off by a lapdog lover. You will require a writer who uses an upright slant and creates wide, even spaces between words.

If you thrive on closeness, a right slant writer is imperative for you. A vertical writer will do, but they will do only if the forms are highly rounded.

And if you crave mutual dependency, find a right slant or extreme right slanter who makes narrow spaces between words.

13. How generous are you?

To a fault—I'll give ya the shirt off my back.

When appropriate.

Money is meant to be invested.

If you're generous to the point of extravagance, you'll probably be turned off by a spendthrift. So look for someone who shares your lavish ways—their writing will show lots of movement and fluidity, wide letters and a widening left margin.

If you pride yourself on thriftiness, then you'll have the highest financial compatibility potential with a writer who keeps well-organized margins and narrow, even spaces between words.

And if you're a tightwad and proud of it, then look for a lover whose writing is narrow and restrained, and who possibly maintains narrow right and left margins.

14. How aggressive are you?

Gentle as the wind.

I get my two cents in when the situation calls for it.

Call me Rambo.

If you're a modest maiden or low-key lad, you'll be intimidated by anyone who *doesn't* have a rounded writing with garland formations and lots of loops.

If you're somewhat aggressive, look for a writing that shows good pressure and good movement to the right.

If you're a born fighter, then you'll probably pick on a partner who doesn't have *your* strong pressure, excellent rightward movement and angular formations.

15. How honest are you?

Honest as the day is long.

Somewhat crafty.

A manipulator—and I'm entitled to be!

If you have a high integrity quotient, then you'll be happiest with someone who has clear forms, good legibility and a lack of confusion between zones.

If you have manipulative tendencies, then you'll meet your match with another thread writer.

And if you're the smoothest of smooth operators whose writing uses both threads and angles, then you will have your lowest compatibility with an ingenuous garland writer, your highest with a thread writer who will challenge you to outfox them!

16. Can you make a commitment?

Isn't that what life is all about?
Not yet.
That word gives me the willies.

If you feel that commitment is your adult responsibility, then you will have the highest commitment compatibility with a writer whose writing is clear and legible, and whose zones are well balanced.

If you're not ready to make a commitment, then seek out a mate whose confused zones show similar searching for a value system.

And if the very word scares you, then look for an irregular writer with an extreme right margin—don't be snared by a schooltype writer with a right slant, strong regularity and good balance between zones!

17. How romantic are you?

A sentimental fool.
A passionate soul.
A brokenhearted cynic.

If you're an incurable romantic, you'll be frustrated with anyone who doesn't have a right slant, rounded letters, garlands and big loops in the upper and/or lower zone.

If passion's your game, you might enjoy the intensity of an obsessive angle writer.

And if you're cynical about love, then study up on your Lovestrokes—sooner or later, you'll recognize Mr. or Ms. Write!

Index

Actors and actresses, signatures of, 114–20
Addictive personalities, 106–7
Aggressiveness, 133
Ainsworth, Mary, 89
Ambitiousness, 128
Angle formations (or connections), 25
  emotional control and, 68
Angular writing, 32, 46
  emotional control and, 69
  of obsessive romantics, 49
  sexuality and, 53–54
Arcade formations (or connections), 25
  emotional control and, 69–70
Athletes, signatures of, 122–23

Baseline, 28
  sexuality and, 56–57
Basic techniques of handwriting analysis, 17–32
  connective forms, 24–26
  extreme formations, 30
  first impressions, 18–19
  ideal handwriting sample for, 17–18
  logic versus intuition, 20
  regularity, 30–31

Basic techniques (*continued*)
  roundness versus angularity, 26–27
  schooltype versus creative handwriting, 19–20
  simplification, 20–21
  slant, 21–24
  Three Zones of Handwriting, 28–29
Brayer, Ruth, 110–12

Capitals
  schooltype, 20, 21
  simplified, 20–21
Castro, Fidel, 123–24
Cautious but generous personality, 108–9
Celebrity signatures, 114–25
Chapman, Mark David, 106
Classic romantics, 47
Commitment, 82–88, 134
  dependent, 85–86
  incapable of, 86–88
  mature, 83–85
  sentimental, 85
Communication of feelings, need for, 128